WORKING
IT
OUT

A Troubleshooting Guide
for Writers

WORKING
IT
OUT

A Troubleshooting Guide
for Writers

Third Edition

Barbara Fine Clouse

Boston   Burr Ridge, IL   Dubuque, IA   Madison, WI   New York   San Francisco   St. Louis
Bangkok   Bogotá   Caracas   Lisbon   London   Madrid
Mexico City   Milan   New Delhi   Seoul   Singapore   Sydney   Taipei   Toronto

McGraw-Hill Higher Education

A Division of The **McGraw-Hill** Companies

WORKING IT OUT: A TROUBLESHOOTING GUIDE FOR WRITERS, THIRD EDITION

This book is printed on acid-free paper.

2 3 4 5 6 7 8 9 0 FGR/FGR 0 9 8 7 6 5 4 3 2

ISBN 0–07–236748–2

Editorial director: *Phillip A. Butcher*
Publisher: *Michael D. Lange*
Senior sponsoring editor: *Sarah Touborg*
Developmental editor: *Alexis Walker*
Marketing manager: *Thayne Conrad*
Project manager: *Kelly L. Delso*
Production supervisor: *Gina Hangos*
Coordinator freelance design: *Mary Christianson*
New media: *Todd Vaccaro*
Freelance Cover designer: *Kay Fulton*
Compositor: *Shepherd, Inc.*
Typeface: 10/12 Melior
Printer: *Quebecor Printing Book Group/ Fairfield*
Cover image: *The Observatory Group*

The credits section for this book begins on page 00 and is considered an extension of the copyright page.

Library of Congress Cataloging-in-Publication Data
Clouse, Barbara Fine.
  Working it out: a troubleshooting guide for writers / Barbara Fine Clouse.-- 3rd ed.
    p. cm.
  Includes index.
  ISBN 07-236748-2 (acid free paper)
  1. English language-- Rhetoric. 2. English language-- Grammar. 3. Report writing. I. Title.
PE1408.C5378 2001
808'.042--dc21   00-027368

When ordering this title, use ISBN 0–07–236748–2

http://www.mhhe.com

In loving memory of Bob Krantz

CONTENTS

xiii
Contents

PREFACE

Working It Out: A Troubleshooting Guide for Writers is a compendium of strategies for handling all aspects of writing: idea generation, outlining, drafting, revising, and editing. It is based on the simple belief that people write better when they discover procedures that work well for them. Thus, one goal of the book is to provide a range of strategies for writers to sample as they work to develop successful writing processes.

A second goal of the book is to help writers when they get stuck. While seasoned writers understand that false starts, wrong turns, and writer's block are all part of the process, less-experienced writers may become frustrated when their work does not proceed smoothly, especially if they do not know what to do when they hit a snag. As a troubleshooting guide, *Working It Out* provides specific strategies for dealing with writing problems. A writer who gets stuck can consult the text and get help.

FEATURES

The features of *Working It Out* aim to make the book an efficient reference for those who want to improve their writing by discovering effective procedures and problem-solving strategies.

Over 240 Helpful Strategies

There are enough specific suggestions here that all users should find many ways to solve problems and improve their writing processes.

Clear, Jargon-Free Prose Written in a Conversational Style

So the book can be a ready reference both in and out of the classroom, explanations are as brief as possible and are written in a supportive, nonintimidating style.

Organization across the Sequence of the Writing Process

Writers can use the text in the same sequence as their writing. Part I treats prewriting; Part II treats drafting; Part III treats revising; and Part IV treats editing. (Part V provides topics for writing practice.)

Chapters Structured as Responses to Questions and Comments Voiced by Student Writers

Students and other novice writers can find what they need faster because chapter titles echo their own language and concerns.

Computer Strategies

A range of strategies is offered for writing at the computer.

An Overview of the Writing Process and Essay Structure

The Introduction contains information on the stages of the writing process; the writer's audience, purpose, and role; essay structure; and strategies for becoming a better writer.

Ideas for Writing

Chapter 26 contains 15 ideas for writing, in full rhetorical context.

Readings Available from the Primis Database

You can design your own book of readings to accompany *Working It Out.* Just visit the Primis website at http://www.mhhe.com/primis/cornerstones and create your own Primis book online! Or, if you prefer, contact your McGraw-Hill sales representative. (If you are not sure who that is, check out McGraw-Hill's sales representative locator at http://www.mhhe.com.)

Helpful Tips for Students and Instructors

Visit the Barbara Clouse website at http://www.mhhe.com/clouse for teaching tips and writing ideas. This website is updated frequently, so stop by often, and feel free to make suggestions for other features you might like to see there.

A Toll-Free Interactive Reader Line

You can make comments or ask questions about *Working It Out* by calling 1-800-435-2672, extension 29315.

New to the Third Edition

The changes made in the third edition of *Working It Out* are in response to suggestions made by student and instructor reviewers and frequent users of the book. These changes include

- The addition of over 50 new strategies, including many new computer strategies.

- New material on essay structure, including a new, argumentation essay to illustrate structure.

- The addition of new chapters, including chapters on writing the thesis, essay organization, and punctuating direct quotations.

- The addition of material on avoiding wordiness, achieving parallelism, and distinguishing homophones.

- New examples to freshen and update the text.

- For better organization, the reconfiguration of some chapters.

Acknowledgments

I am grateful to Sarah Touborg and Alexis Walker of McGraw-Hill, for their support and guidance. In addition, I owe much to the sound counsel of the following reviewers, whose insights inform this book:

Barbara E. Beale
California State University, Fullerton

Bradford Crain
College of the Ozarks

John Green
Salem State College

Howard Hopkins
Lansing Community College

Brian Kennedy
Pasadena City College

Charles Kerlin
Saint Joseph's College

Patrick Mathias
Itasca Community College

Andrea Shanklin
Howard Community College

Jill Widner
Yakima Valley Community College

Finally, to my understanding husband, Denny, and to my delightful children, Greg and Jeff, I offer thanks for the support and for the room of my own.

First Things First: An Introduction
"Do I Have to Buy the Book?"

College instructors expect certain questions on the first day of class, questions like "Is the final comprehensive?" "Do you count attendance?" "Do you test on the book or on the lectures?" "Is there a curve?" And sometimes even, "Do we have to buy the book?" By explaining how this book can help you become a better writer and by providing important preliminary information, this chapter aims to make you glad that you took out your wallet.

How to Use *Working It Out: A Troubleshooting Guide for Writers*

Pretend for a moment that you play tennis and that you are having trouble with your baseline shots. A coach, noticing your problem, might suggest that you drop your hip a little. Now pretend that you are a serious runner and you are having trouble improving your time in the 1,600 meter run. In this case, your coach might suggest that you swing your arms more and pretend a giant hand is on your back pushing you along. That's what coaches do: They make suggestions to help you solve problems that arise as a natural part of learning to do something better.

Right now, you are working to become a better writer, and as you do, problems will arise from time to time. Do not let these problems worry you, for they are a natural part of the learning process. Whenever we try to learn something, we hit snags now and then. The point is that we need to discover how to *solve* problems—and that is a learning experience of its own.

As you work to become a better writer, think of this book as one of your coaches. If you encounter a problem, look to this book for one or more suggestions for solving that problem. Of course, this book is not your only coach. Your classroom teacher is the best coach of all, and your classmates and the tutors in the writing center are also good sources of information. So if you have a problem, you can also talk to one of these people to get

1

suggestions for overcoming the obstacle. Ask them what specific procedures they follow, and try some of them to see if they work well for you too.

To use this book efficiently, do the following:

- Read over the table of contents so you have a sense of what the book covers. Notice that most of the chapters are titled with a remark often spoken by struggling writers.

- If you get stuck when you are writing, go back to the table of contents and find the remark that best expresses the problem you are having. Turn to the chapter titled with that remark.

- Quickly read the chapter (it will be short), and notice that a number of procedures are described for helping you overcome the obstacle. Pick the procedure that appeals to you the most and try it. If your problem is solved, great. If not, try another procedure. Some procedures will work for you and some will not because different strategies will be effective for different personal styles. If after trying three procedures you have not solved the problem, talk things over with your classroom teacher or a writing center tutor. *You are not expected to try every procedure each time you work through a chapter.*

- If you are not having any problems but want to discover more effective or efficient procedures, read through the book with an eye toward procedures to try the next time you write.

As you work to become a better writer, remember that following the procedures in this book will not guarantee complete success. These procedures are problem-solving strategies meant to ease the way. No set of procedures can guarantee success, but the ones in this book can help you to your goal.

HOW TO BECOME A BETTER WRITER

Becoming a better writer has much in common with becoming a better swimmer, becoming a better piano player, or becoming a better dancer. In all these cases, a person is working to improve a skill. As you work to improve your writing skills, remember the following.

1. **Be patient.** Improving a skill takes time. Just as perfecting a foul shot takes a basketball player time and practice, so too will improving your writing. If you expect too much too soon, you will become frustrated. So set reasonable goals by looking for slow, steady progress rather than dramatic, overnight improvement.

2. **Expect to get stuck.** Everyone does, even experienced, professional writers. Writer's block and dead ends are all part of writing, so do not

think there is something wrong with you if you have some trouble. Consult this text, your instructor, other experienced writers, and/or a writing center tutor when you get stuck. When you solve the problem, tuck the solution away for future reference, so the same problem does not plague you over and over again.

3. **Remember that writing is really rewriting.** Experienced writers work and rework drafts a number of times before they are satisfied. With each revision, you will learn a little more about writing, so welcome rewrites as learning opportunities, and know that you are acting like an experienced writer each time you revise.

4. **Be aware of what you do when you write.** Decide which procedures work well for you and which do not. Then consult this text and your instructor for procedures to replace ones that did not work. For example, maybe idea generation goes well for you, but revision does not. That means you need to discover new revision procedures. When your procedures work better, your writing will improve.

5. **Talk to other writers.** Find out what they do when they write, and try some of their procedures. When you need ideas, talk to others and kick around possibilities. Share your frustrations and successes. Form a network with your classmates and other writers for support and suggestions. You can help each other improve.

6. **Study the responses to your writing.** What does your instructor say about your writing? What do your classmates say when they read your drafts? What do people in the writing center say? Reader response is valuable to a writer. By paying attention to this response and working to improve areas where readers see weaknesses, you can improve more quickly. If you do not understand a response made by your instructor or another reader, or if you do not know how to make a change, ask for help.

7. **Read, read, read.** Read every day—the newspaper, your textbooks, newsmagazines, short stories, novels. Read anything that interests you. Pay attention to how other writers handle introductions, conclusions, supporting detail, and transitions. Look up unfamiliar words, notice sentence structure, and observe punctuation. Try to incorporate strategies that you observe in your reading into some of your writing. The more you read, the more you will internalize about the nature of language, and the faster your writing will improve. Furthermore, frequent reading makes you more knowledgeable, so you have more ideas for your writing.

8. **Do not fear mistakes.** They are a natural part of learning. Go ahead and give your writing your best shot. Take risks; try things out. If you make mistakes, embrace them as opportunities to learn. If you are

afraid of making a mistake, you will never try; if you never try, you will never grow.

Myths about Writing

People believe many things about writing—and much of what they believe is not true. Following is a list of commonly believed myths about writing. If you are surprised to learn that the "facts" listed are untrue, check the chapter indicated for the accurate information.

Myth	Accurate Information
Writers are born, not made.	Introduction
"Good" writers rarely struggle.	Introduction
Writers should wait for inspiration.	Chapter 1
"Good" writers get it right the first time.	Chapters 4–15
"Good" writers write fast.	Chapters 9–15
Outlining is very time-consuming.	Chapter 3
Introductions should be written first.	Chapter 5
The best conclusions summarize the main points.	Chapter 7
The longer the words, the better they are.	Chapter 8
The longer the writing, the better it is.	Chapter 13
Revising involves reading over a draft and fixing spelling and punctuation.	Chapter 10
Only English teachers understand grammar rules.	Chapters 16–25
Sentence fragments are always short.	Chapter 17
Run-ons and comma splices are always long.	Chapter 18
Use a comma wherever you pause in speech.	Chapter 22
There are no rules to explain English spelling.	Chapter 25

The Writing Process

Like many people, you may think that a "good" writer can produce an effective piece in a minimum amount of time with very little effort. If you do, you are mistaken, for successful writers typically work and rework their pieces through the following time-consuming series of stages:

1. Prewriting
2. Drafting

3. Revising

4. Editing

Let's look at what each of these stages involves.

Prewriting

If you sit around waiting for inspiration before you write, you may never get anything written. You see, inspiration does not occur often enough for writers to depend on it. In fact, inspiration occurs so rarely that writers must develop other means for getting their ideas. Collectively, the procedures for coming up with ideas in the absence of inspiration are called *prewriting*. The term *prewriting* is used because these procedures come before writing the first draft.

Chapters 1–3 describe procedures for coming up with ideas to write about and for discovering ways to order those ideas. If you follow some of these procedures, you can avoid staring at a blank page waiting for inspiration that may never come.

Drafting

Once writers have generated enough ideas during prewriting to serve as a departure point, they make their first attempt at getting those ideas down. This part of the writing process is *drafting*. Typically, the first draft is very rough, which is why it so often is called the *rough draft*. The rough draft provides raw material that can be shaped and refined in the next stages of the writing process. Chapters 4–8 describe procedures you can try when you draft.

Revising

Revising calls on the writer to take the raw material of the draft and rework it to get it in shape for the reader. This reworking is a time-consuming, difficult part of the process. It requires the writer to refine the content so that it is clear, so that points are adequately supported, and so that ideas are expressed in the best way possible and in the best order possible. The procedures described in Chapters 9–15 can help you when you revise.

Editing

Because experienced readers will expect your writing to be free of errors, you have a responsibility to *edit* to find and eliminate mistakes so that they do not distract or annoy your reader. However, many writers hunt for errors too soon, before they have revised for the larger concerns of content and effective expression. Editing should really be saved for the end of the process. When you are ready to edit, the procedures in Chapters 16–25 can help you.

Writing Does Not Progress in a Straight Line

Writers do not always move in a straight line from prewriting to drafting to revising to editing. Instead, they often double back before going forward. For example, while drafting you may think of a new idea to add, so you have left drafting and doubled back to prewriting. While editing you may think of a better way to phrase an idea, so you have left editing and doubled back to revising. Never consider any stage of the process "done" and behind you. Always stand ready to go back to an earlier stage when a good idea strikes you.

Developing Your Own Writing Process

Although we have been talking about "the" writing process, there really is no single, correct process. Instead, writers develop procedures that work well for them, so that every successful writer can have a different, successful process. As you use this book and work to become a better writer, try a range of procedures for prewriting, drafting, revising, and editing. Some of these procedures will work well for you and some will not. Continue sampling until you have strategies for handling all the stages of writing, and at that point you will have discovered your own successful process.

THE CONTEXT FOR WRITING

Circumstances influence everything we do—including writing. Even if you are writing just a grocery list, circumstances such as how much money you have, what the store specials are, what produce is in season, and what you like to eat will influence what you put on your list. Are you doing the shopping, or is a friend doing it for you? If you are the one who must read the list, you might abbreviate heavily and write sloppily, but if someone else must read it, then you probably will abbreviate less and write more legibly. Are you in a hurry? If so, you might arrange your list according to the way the food aisles are set up so you can get in and out quickly. Yes, circumstances influence even the simplest writing task.

Three circumstances influence the writer enough that they form the *context* for writing. These factors are

1. The writer's purpose

2. The writer's audience

3. The writer's role

The pages that follow will explain these three circumstances. If you need help identifying them for your own writing, see "Identify Your Writing Context" on page 28.

The Writer's Purpose

Even when you write something as basic and simple as a shopping list, you have a *purpose* for your writing: You want to be sure that you do not forget to buy anything. Similarly, all writing is written for a specific purpose.

Sometimes writers want to *relate an experience,* perhaps to express feelings or perhaps to aid reflection. For example, if you interviewed for a research position in the biology lab, you might write an e-mail to a friend to tell about the experience and how nervous you are about your performance. Or you might write about the experience in your journal or diary as a way to consider what happened and evaluate your performance.

Some writing is meant to *inform* a reader, perhaps to increase the reader's knowledge, perhaps to provide a record, or perhaps to help the reader in some way. For example, a magazine article about cholesterol can increase a reader's understanding of how this substance affects the body; the proceedings of government agencies can be written into logs, archives, and official records to serve as a permanent record; the owner's manual for a VCR can provide information to help the reader operate the device.

Some writing aims to *persuade* a reader to think or act a particular way. For example, a newspaper editorial endorsing a political candidate is written to convince the reader to vote for that candidate.

Finally, some writing, like a short story in a literary magazine, aims to *entertain* the reader. Of course, writing can have more than one purpose, as when you tell a story both to entertain the reader and to relate an experience.

In short, there are four common purposes for writing:

1. To relate experience

2. To inform

3. To persuade

4. To entertain

Your purpose for writing will affect what you say and how you say it. For example, assume that you just bought a new home, and you want to write about the experience. To *relate experience,* you could tell what happened when you purchased the home and include emotional details about the stress and frustration you experienced. To *inform,* you could explain how a prospective home buyer can evaluate the condition of a house and include specific details about procedures to follow. To *persuade,* you could argue that laws are needed to protect home buyers from unscrupulous real estate agents, and you could include what the laws should state and the reasons they are needed. To *entertain,* you could write a humorous piece about moving day and include exaggerated, funny details about your misadventures. Of course, you can also combine purposes, which will affect your detail accordingly.

The Writer's Audience and Role

Your *audience* (the person or people who will read your writing) is the second element that forms the context for writing, because your reader influences what you say and how you say it. For example, say that you need to borrow $100 to get through the month because you did not live within your budget. If you were e-mailing a close friend to request the loan, your writing would be relaxed and informal. You might not even explain why you have come up short or when you will repay the money. Part of your writing might be something like this:

To...	Frazier, Dale
Cc...	
Subject:	help!

Hey, Dale –

I hate to do this to you, buddy, but I need a hundred bucks fast – never mind why. I'll get it back to you as soon as I can.

Lee

If you were writing a note to your parents, you would be a little more formal and forthcoming about why you need the money and how you will pay it back:

My phone bill was higher than I expected, so I've come up short this month. I'm really sorry—I've learned my lesson about calling Jan every day. I plan to work overtime three days next week, so I know I can repay the loan after my next paycheck.

How your reader feels about you will also influence your detail and word choice. For example, consider a letter to convince your parents, who love you, to loan you $100 and one to persuade your boss to advance you the money. How might the detail and word choice for these two pieces of writing differ?

Similarly, your detail and word choice will be affected by your reader's situation. For example, assume you are writing to convince your reader that a longer school year is a good idea. If your audience includes working mothers, you might mention that a longer school year will cut down on child-care hassles. However, if your audience includes teenagers, this argument would mean little. Instead, you might note that they would be more competitive when they apply for admission into college.

One way to gear your detail and word choice to your audience is to complete a reader profile to get a sense of your reader's makeup. Such a profile can be like the one on pages 77–78.

Perhaps you are thinking that if you are in a writing class your audience will be your writing instructor. Keep in mind, however, that writing teachers can assume the identities of different audiences so you can practice writing for a range of readers.

The flipside of audience is the writer's *role.* If your role is that of a student writing for a teacher, you will be careful to conform to all the terms of the assignment. If your role is that of an employee writing for a boss, you will work to sound polite and competent. If your role is that of a friend, your word choice might be informal; it may even include slang. However, if your role is that of a job applicant, you will avoid slang.

The Intersection of Audience and Purpose

The way audience and purpose come together dramatically affects the context for writing. For example, two pieces of writing that have the same purpose will be very different if written for different audiences. Consider the recruitment letters sent out by your college admissions office. A letter aimed at recruiting a star high school athlete may highlight one aspect of your college, while a letter aimed at a prospective theater major may highlight a different aspect. Similarly, pieces written for the same audience but with different purposes will also be different. Consider two letters sent out by your school's alumni office to recent graduates. A letter inviting the graduates to join the alumni association will be very different from one urging the graduates to make a contribution to the school.

Three Writing Tasks, Three Contexts.   Assume that you borrowed your brother's car and that while it was parked someone sideswiped it, causing extensive damage. Now assume you have three writing tasks ahead of you:

1.   Leaving your brother a note explaining what happened to the car.

2.   Writing your parents to explain what happened so you can borrow money to have the car fixed.

3.   Writing your friend who attends another school to tell that person what happened.

How will these three pieces of writing differ? In what ways will the writer's context be responsible for those differences?

ESSAY STRUCTURE

Essay structure refers to the way an essay is put together. You already know the most basic fact about essay structure: an essay has a beginning, a middle, and an end.

The Introduction

The opening paragraph (and in some cases, paragraphs) is the *introduction*. The introduction is important because readers often decide right there whether or not to read on, so writers must craft introductions geared to stimulate a reader's interest. Suggestions for ways to engage a reader's interest appear in Chapter 5, and now would be a good time to skim that material.

In addition to creating interest, a good introduction often includes the *thesis,* which is the sentence or sentences expressing the writer's assertion about the topic under consideration. A good thesis presents an idea worth writing about—something that is disputed or in need of explanation.

Acceptable thesis:	Although everyone agrees that children must be adequately cared for, this country does not properly regulate day-care centers.
Explanation:	The thesis idea is open to debate and in need of explanation.
Unacceptable thesis:	Children must be adequately cared for.
Explanation:	No one will disagree with the thesis idea, so why bother writing about it?
Acceptable thesis:	Rose Lewin, my grandmother, is a woman of courage and determination.
Explanation:	The thesis idea is in need of explanation.
Unacceptable thesis:	Rose Lewin is my grandmother.
Explanation:	The thesis idea is a statement of fact that requires no explanation; no one would dispute it.

For more on the thesis, see Chapter 2.

To give you an idea of how an introduction can stimulate interest and present the thesis, here is a simple introduction taken from the essay on page 15.

Material creates interest with list of problems in schools, warning about the complexity of the issue, and a brief analysis of the proposed solution.

Right now, something is terribly wrong in our public schools: test scores are down, attendance is dropping, violence is increasing, students are bored and angst-ridden, teachers are demoralized, and parents are frustrated, angry, and worried. Because the problems are multifaceted, the solutions are likely to be complex. However, many are still looking to the quick fix, in this case wearing school uniforms. Uniforms have long been worn by students in private schools, but lately more people are calling for them in public schools. Advocates claim that uniforms will solve everything from low self-esteem and poor grades to minor discipline problems and outbursts of serious violence. When pressed to back up their claims, however, the advocates can do little more than cite anecdotal evidence, because there is no proof that uniforms accomplish all that some say they do. <u>In short, requiring public school students to wear uniforms will not solve the complex problems that plague our public schools.</u> Other means of solving our educational problems must be found.

Underlined sentence is the thesis. It notes that the essay will argue that uniforms will not solve the problems in public schools.

The Body Paragraphs

Your reader will not believe your thesis unless you <u>prove</u> it to be true. Does your thesis state that schools should teach conflict resolution? Then you have to provide solid reasons why this is a good idea. Does your thesis state that high-protein weight-loss diets can be dangerous? Then you must explain how the diets can be harmful. Does your thesis state that the new education building is an eyesore? Then you need to describe the unattractive features of the building. And that is where the body paragraphs come in. The *body paragraphs* present the ideas that prove or explain your thesis idea, so your reader will accept the truth of the thesis.

The Structure of Body Paragraphs. Body paragraphs typically have two parts: the topic sentence and the supporting details. The *topic sentence* is the sentence (or sometimes two) that presents the focus of the body paragraph, the particular point that will be made and developed to back up the thesis. The other part of a body paragraph is formed by the *supporting details.* These are the ideas you write to explain or develop the topic sentence. Just as a reader will not believe your thesis unless you show that it is true, a reader will not believe your topic sentence unless you provide proof. The points you make in body paragraphs are often called *supporting details* because they are <u>details</u> that <u>support</u> the topic sentence idea, which, in turn, supports the thesis.

In most cases, each body paragraph develops only one point in support of the thesis, so each topic sentence presents only one idea. Sometimes the topic sentence is the first sentence in the paragraph or near the first, and sometimes it is last or near the end. When you place the topic sentence first or nearly first, you give your reader an upfront statement of the point you will develop in support of the thesis, and then you go on to provide supporting details to prove that point. When you place your topic sentence last or nearly last, your supporting details provide specific evidence that leads to the conclusion stated in the topic sentence. Here are two paragraphs that illustrate the structure of body paragraphs, taken from the essay on page 15. The topic sentences are underlined; notice their different placement.

> The supporting details give evidence leading to the conclusion stated in the topic sentence.

Unlike private schools, public schools cannot require students to wear uniforms. Certainly, public schools can establish and enforce reasonable dress codes, but because the Constitution guarantees everyone's right to a public education, those who object to wearing uniforms for religious or other compelling reasons cannot be kept out of school. This means that public schools can do little more than <u>urge</u> students to wear uniforms. If many choose not to, what is accomplished? If some students wear uniforms and others do not, the chances are good that the two groups of students will be treated differently by teachers and administrators. They will likely give preferential treatment to those who wear the recommended uniforms. After all, these are the students that teachers and administrators favor, the ones who do as they are told. Those who choose not to wear uniforms can easily become second-class citizens because they will be perceived as the trouble-makers, as the ones who do not follow the rules. <u>Thus, uniforms in public schools are likely to create a two-tiered caste system and promote preferential treatment.</u>

> Each topic sentence presents one point to develop the thesis, and each presents the focus of the body paragraph.

<u>Perhaps more important is the fact that a school-uniform policy eliminates opportunity for self-expression.</u> The elimination of self-expression is worrisome because school already demands so much conformity: everyone takes the same classes, keeps the same hours, chooses from the same activities, behaves according to the same rules, and learns the same material. School should help young people express their individuality and creativity so they become comfortable with their personal styles and learn to appreciate the differences around them, but how can they do that if everything about the institution calls for conformity? Allowing students to choose what to wear affords them a harmless respite from the conformity inherent in so much of public education.

> The supporting details work to develop the topic sentence.

Sometimes the topic sentence is not stated at all; instead, it is strongly implied by the supporting details. For an example of a body paragraph with an implied topic sentence, see paragraph 4 of the essay on page 15.

Supporting Detail

Because you must *prove* the truth of your thesis and topic sentences, your supporting details must be *adequate,* which means you must have enough of them to prove or explain the thesis and each topic sentence to your reader's satisfaction. To appreciate the importance of adequate detail, read the following body paragraph, which does *not* have adequate detail.

> Proponents of school uniforms say that the uniforms offer a range of benefits to students. They say that uniforms reduce gang influence, that they minimize violence by reducing some of the sources of conflict among students, and that they help identify those who are trespassing on school property. It is true that gang affiliation can be signaled by clothing and that students have been attacked because of what they wear. However, uniforms will not necessarily address this problem. There will always be ways to mark status and group affiliation, so that source of conflict will always be present. As for trespassers, much of the serious violence in schools is begun by the students themselves, not by trespassers.

Notice how much more convincing the following paragraph is because of the more substantial supporting details.

> Proponents of school uniforms say that the uniforms offer a range of benefits to students. They say that uniforms reduce gang influence, that they minimize violence by reducing some of the sources of conflict among students, and that they help identify those who are trespassing on school property. It is true that gang affiliation can be signaled by clothing and that students have been attacked because of what they wear. However, uniforms will not necessarily address this problem because students are still free to wear jewelry, watches, shoes, and coats for which they can be the targets of violence. They can also carry backpacks, ride bikes, and drive cars that can create tensions leading to violence. There will always be ways to mark status and group affiliation, so that source of conflict will always be present. As for trespassers, school officials, teachers, and security guards know who does and does not belong on school grounds, and if they do not, then identification cards can be issued to address the problem. Further, much of the serious violence in schools is begun by the students themselves, not by trespassers.

Writers have many strategies for providing adequate detail, including describing, telling a story, giving examples, explaining causes and/or effects, showing similarities and/or differences, and showing how something is made or done. (For more on strategies for providing adequate detail, see Chapter 6.)

In addition to being adequate, supporting details must be *relevant,* which means they must be directly related to both the thesis and the topic sentence of the paragraph they appear in. For example, a paragraph with the topic sentence, "Perhaps more important is the fact that a school-uniform policy takes away choice" should not include detail about whether or not uniforms improve grades. This detail is not relevant to the topic sentence, and including it will distract and sidetrack your reader.

Finally, body paragraphs and supporting details should be presented in a *logical order,* perhaps one of the following:

- In order of importance (from the least significant to the most significant point)—An essay arguing against restricting immigration might begin with the least compelling reasons and move on to the most compelling reasons.

- In time order (from the first event to the last event)—A story can begin with the first event and proceed in sequence to the last event.

- From general to specific (from a general statement to specific examples) or from specific to general (from specific examples to general statements)—An essay explaining the value of a liberal arts education can first state that a liberal arts education makes a person versatile, and then give specific examples of that versatility. Or it can first give examples of the benefits of a liberal arts education and then conclude with the statement that the education makes a person versatile.

- In order across space (from near to far, front to back, left to right, and so forth)—A real estate brochure describing a house can arrange details from room to room.

- In a problem–solution order (a statement of a problem followed by an explanation of a solution)—A magazine article about Americans' lack of physical fitness might first explain the problem and then offer suggestions for solving it.

- In a cause-and-effect order (an explanation of why an event occurs followed by an explanation of the results of that event)—A research paper about the Nixon presidency could give the causes of the Watergate scandal and go on to note the effects of the scandal on American politics.

The Conclusion

The end of an essay is the *conclusion.* Conclusions are important very simply because final impressions are important. To realize this, think back to the last movie or television show you watched that ended badly. Remember how let down you felt? Writers do not want to leave their readers feeling let down because a negative final impression can undermine the effectiveness of the entire essay. Instead, writers aim to provide a sense of closure, a sense of comfortable completeness—like that provided in this conclusion from the essay below.

> The problems in our schools mirror problems in the larger society, and these problems must be addressed. Courses in conflict resolution, programs to help students elevate their self-esteem, additional extracurricular activities, and secure schools will go a long way to solving the problems. School uniforms, however, are likely to create more problems than they solve.

A Sample Essay

The sample paragraphs in the preceding sections were taken from the essay that follows. As you read, pay attention to structure. (The thesis and topic sentences are underlined as a study aid.)

The Uniform Solution

The *introduction* creates interest with a sense of urgency that comes from words like "terribly wrong" and "angst-ridden." It also gives helpful background information by noting the beliefs of people who favor uniforms.

The thesis is a very direct statement of the author's point of view and the essay's focus.

Note the use of words like "however" and "in short" to link sentences. (See p. 87 on transitions.)

[1]Right now, something is terribly wrong in our public schools: test scores are down, attendance is dropping, violence is increasing, students are bored and angst-ridden, teachers are demoralized, and parents are frustrated, angry, and worried. Because the problems are multifaceted, the solutions are likely to be complex. However, many are still looking to the quick fix, in this case wearing school uniforms. Uniforms have long been worn by students in private schools, but lately more people are calling for them in public schools. Advocates claim that uniforms will solve everything from low self-esteem and poor grades to minor discipline problems and outbursts of serious violence. When pressed to back up their claims, however, the advocates can do little more than cite anecdotal evidence, because there is no proof that uniforms accomplish all that some say they do. In short, requiring public school students to wear uniforms will not solve the complex problems that plague our public schools. Other means of solving our educational problems must be found.

In *paragraph 2*, note the cause-and-effect order. The cause is constitutional guarantee of public education; the effect is that uniforms cannot be required. Another cause is that some students do not wear uniforms; the effect is preferential treatment.

The paragraph is convincing because many will react strongly to the threat of preferential treatment.

²Unlike private schools, public schools cannot require students to wear uniforms. Certainly, public schools can establish and enforce reasonable dress codes, but because the Constitution guarantees everyone's right to a public education, those who object to wearing uniforms for religious or other compelling reasons cannot be kept out of school. This means that public schools can do little more than <u>urge</u> students to wear uniforms. If many choose not to, what is accomplished? If some students wear uniforms and others do not, the chances are good that the two groups of students will be treated differently by teachers and administrators. They will likely give preferential treatment to those who wear the recommended uniforms. After all, these are the students that teachers and administrators favor, the ones who do as they are told. Those who choose not to wear uniforms can easily become second-class citizens because they will be perceived as the trouble-makers, as the ones who do not follow the rules. <u>Thus, uniforms in public schools are likely to create a two-tiered caste system and promote preferential treatment.</u>

In *paragraph 3* note the linking of ideas with the phrase "perhaps more important" and that the author explains why the topic sentence idea of self-expression is important. Therefore, a reason is stated <u>and</u> explained.

³<u>Perhaps more important is the fact that a school-uniform policy eliminates opportunity for self-expression.</u> The elimination of self-expression is worrisome because school already demands so much conformity: everyone takes the same classes, keeps the same hours, chooses from the same activities, behaves according to the same rules, and learns the same material. School should help young people express their individuality and creativity so they become comfortable with their personal styles and learn to appreciate the differences around them, but how can they do that if everything about the institution calls for conformity? Allowing students to choose what to wear affords them a harmless respite from the conformity inherent in so much of public education.

The topic sentence of *paragraph 4* is implied: the arguments of those who favor uniforms are not strong. The supporting detail lets the reader know that the writer is aware of the

⁴Proponents of school uniforms say that the uniforms offer a range of benefits to students. They say that uniforms reduce gang influence, that they minimize violence by reducing some of the sources of conflict among students, and that they help identify those who are trespassing on school property. It is true that gang affiliation can be signaled by clothing and that students have been attacked because of what they wear. However, uniforms will not necessarily address this problem because students are still free to wear jewelry, watches, shoes, and coats for which they can be the targets of violence. They can also carry backpacks, ride bikes, and drive cars that can create tensions leading to violence. There will always be ways to mark status and group affiliation, so that source of conflict

opposing view. The paragraph gets its convincing quality from the undermining of the opposing view. Note that the author attacks opposing arguments without being nasty or unfair.

In *paragraph 5*, the first two sentences present the topic sentence idea in support of the thesis (the cost of savings with uniforms does not offset the drawbacks). The detail is arranged in a cause-and-effect pattern.

The first three sentences of *paragraph 6* form the topic sentence idea. The supporting details are not very substantial. What kinds of details could be added?

The *conclusion* provides closure by suggesting alternatives to uniforms and by restating the thesis idea that uniforms are not a good idea.

will always be present. As for trespassers, school officials, teachers, and security guards know who does and does not belong on school grounds, and if they do not, then identification cards can be issued to address the problem. Further, much of the serious violence in schools is begun by the students themselves, not by trespassers.

⁵Another argument cited in favor of uniforms is the reduced cost of buying school clothes, once the need to purchase the latest fashion is eliminated. This benefit is probably real, but it does not offset the drawbacks of uniforms, particularly students' loss of the freedom to express themselves and the ability to exert their independence in harmless ways. After all, students express their personalities and independence in the way they dress. Deprive them of that means of expression, and they will find another, perhaps more dramatic way to exert their independence, including tattoos, body piercing, and drug use. Yes, some of that does go on today even without uniforms, but the practices are likely to increase if students are denied a less harmful means of self-expression.

⁶Proponents of uniforms are also fond of noting that they take a great deal of pressure off of students because they eliminate the stress associated with dressing to keep up with others. This is probably true. However, it may not be desirable to eliminate this form of stress. Sure, while they are in school, students can avoid the stress of "competitive dressing." However, once out of school, they may actually be at a disadvantage because they never learned how to deal with this aspect of a competitive social environment and how to be at peace with themselves, regardless of their manner of dress. In college and in the workplace, they will be confronted with the very stress they could avoid in high school. Only now the stakes are higher and the coping strategies are not in place. In short, how will students learn if school officials force everyone to look alike?

⁷The problems in our schools mirror problems in the larger society, and these problems must be addressed. Courses in conflict resolution, programs to help students elevate their self-esteem, additional extracurricular activities, and secure schools will go a long way to solving the problems. School uniforms are likely to create more problems than they solve.

PREWRITING

Before drafting, you should lay some groundwork by discovering something about what you want to say and the order you can say it in. This groundwork is known as prewriting. *Without prewriting, you can find yourself staring for prolonged periods at a blank page. Or you can find yourself beginning, wadding up the paper, beginning again, wadding up more paper, and on and on. The chapters in this section can help you avoid this frustration and waste of time. They describe strategies for discovering ideas you can write about and ways to order those ideas.*

1

"I Don't Know What to Write."

THE TERROR OF THE BLANK PAGE! No, it's not a movie coming soon to a theater near you. It's the fear writers experience when they sit down to write and cannot think of anything to say. Sure, sometimes writers are zapped by the lightning bolt of inspiration, and idea after idea comes tumbling forth. However, inspiration is fickle and cannot be counted on to show up just because you have an essay due a week from Friday. Therefore, if inspiration fails you, take steps to develop ideas on your own. The following strategies, known as *idea generation techniques,* can help you come up with ideas when inspiration does not arrive on time.

Try Freewriting

The act of writing stimulates thought, so when you cannot think of anything to write, start writing anyway. Eventually, ideas will surface.

Freewriting is an idea generation technique that lets you use writing to discover ideas to write about. It works like this: Sit in a quiet spot and write nonstop for about 10 minutes. Record every idea that occurs to you, no matter how silly or irrelevant it may seem. Do not stop for any reason; just keep your pen moving. If you run out of ideas, write the days of the week, names of your family members, even "I don't know what to write." Write *anything.* Soon new thoughts will strike you, and you can write about them.

The important thing about freewriting is to be *free,* so make wild statements, write silly notions, or make random associations. Do not evaluate the worth of anything; if it occurs to you, write it down. Do not worry about grammar, spelling, punctuation, or neatness—just write ideas the best way you can without worrying over anything.

Here is a freewriting produced to discover ideas for an essay about the effects of computers:

> Computers are wonderful and scarry at the same time. They are great because they make things easier and faster, like writing things and getting info. Lets see, what else? They store info and trade it with other computers so our privacy can be invaded, that's pretty scarry. Lap top computers are big now, you see people use them everywhere. That's good and bad because you can work when its convenient but you also work when you should be resting. This whole Internet thing is wierd. People spend whole days on it. Is that productive or lost time? What else? 1 2 3 4 5 6 7 8 Pornography is a problem on the Internet and kids can get involved. Yuk. Now what else? I'm stuck, I'm stuck. If you don't understand computers, you will have trouble in the job market. I guess that means schools better do a good job of teaching this stuff. Now what? Anything else? Expensive. Who can afford all this computer equipment? Is it just for the rich? I read an articel that said computers are changing the way we communicate. I don't remember what all it said, I should look it up.

Note that the freewriting unearthed a number of ideas for an essay about the effects of computers: convenience, possible invasion of privacy, changes in the way people work, the time spent on the Internet, changes in the way people communicate, the need for schools to educate children in computer skills, whether or not computer access is just for the rich. Obviously, these are too many points for one essay, so the writer would narrow things down to one topic.

TRY LOOPING

Looping allows you to explore a topic in more depth by doing a second and sometimes third freewriting. For example, the previous freewriting on the effects of computers yielded several ideas for writing, including "the time spent on the Internet." To try looping, you would freewrite on this topic for 10 minutes to see what emerged. That second "loop" may yield enough material, or you may freewrite a third loop on an idea that emerged in the second loop. Taken together, all the freewriting loops can bring forth considerable material.

TRY CLUSTERING

Clustering is a powerful idea generation technique because it lets you see at a glance how ideas relate to one another. To cluster, write in the middle of a page a subject area you want to think about. Then draw a circle around the subject, so you have something that looks like this:

Next, as you think of ideas, connect them to the central circle to get something like this:

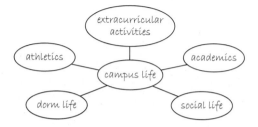

As more ideas occur to you, connect them to the appropriate circles (the ones with ideas the new ideas are most closely related to) to get something like this:

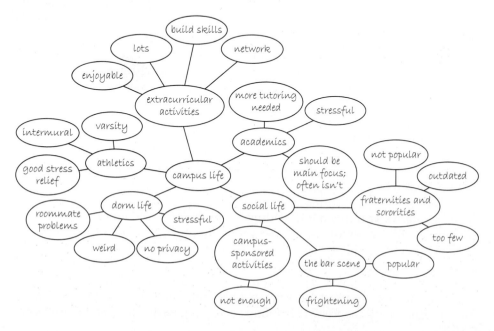

Continue writing ideas and joining them to circles until you can think of nothing else. When you can think of nothing else, study your clustering to see if one particular circle with its connecting circles gives you enough to begin a draft. For example, this portion of the previous clustering might serve as a departure point for a draft about the benefits of extracurricular activities.

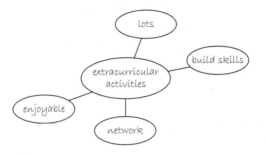

If this clustering does not yield enough ideas for a draft, try yet another clustering to expand the branches:

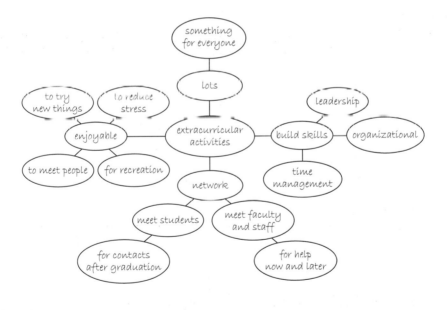

TRY LISTING

An idea generation list records ideas that occur to you in phrases rather than sentences. To be successful at listing, do not censor yourself; write everything you think of. Even if you are sure an idea is terrible, get it down anyway because it may prompt you to think of another, more worthy idea. Here is an idea generation list for an essay about the effects of being cut from the freshman basketball team:

felt rejected

was embarrassed

disappointed my father

got teased

felt inadequate

gave up basketball forever

decided to go out for cross-country

lost my best friend, who was busy with the team

Next, review your list and cross out ideas you do not want to use and add new ideas that occur to you. A benefit of listing is that by numbering the ideas in the list in the order you want to treat them in your draft, you can easily develop a scratch outline.

Sometimes you may wish to write a second list focusing on only one of the points in your first list. For example, a second list focusing on "lost my best friend, who was busy with the team" could look like this:

Cal had no time for me

practiced every day

couldn't go out at night because of curfew

socialized with his teammates

wouldn't play sports with me because of fear of injuries

TRY BRAINSTORMING

To brainstorm for ideas, ask yourself questions about your topic. The answers can provide details for your essay. Sometimes the question that offers up the most is the simple question "Why?" In addition, you may find the following questions helpful:

Why did it happen?	What is it different from?
How did it happen?	What are its physical
Who was involved?	characteristics?
When did it happen?	Why is it important?

Where did it happen?	Who would care about it?
Could it happen again?	What causes it?
What does it mean?	What are its effects?
How does it work?	What is it related to?
Why does this matter to me?	What examples are there?
Why does this matter to my reader?	How can it be explained?
Why is it true?	What controversies are
What is it similar to?	associated with it?

EXAMINE YOUR TOPIC FROM DIFFERENT ANGLES

If you have a broad subject area you want to write about, but you are not sure how to approach or limit the subject, try viewing it from different angles. Asking yourself the following questions can help you see how to approach your topic from different perspectives:

1. **How can I describe my subject?** What does it look, smell, taste, sound, and feel like? What are its parts, its color, its size, its shape, and so on?

2. **How can I compare and contrast my subject?** What is it like, and what is it different from? Are the similarities and differences important?

3. **What do I associate my subject with?** What does it make people think of? What is it related to? What does it develop from or lead to?

4. **How can I analyze my subject?** How is it broken down? How does it work? What is it made of? Why is it important? Is it part of something bigger?

5. **How can I apply my subject?** What is it good for? Who would find it useful? When is it useful? Does it have social, economic, or political value?

6. **What arguments accompany my subject?** What are the reasons for it? What are the reasons against it? Who is for it? Who is against it? Is it right or wrong? Good or bad? How does it affect society?

After answering these questions, you may have an approach to your subject. Then you can do some additional idea generation for ideas to suit your approach.

USE QUESTIONNAIRES

Sometimes it helps to learn what other people think because their ideas can expose you to fresh perspectives and stimulate your own thinking. To discover what others think, you can develop a questionnaire for people to complete. This is not a scientific instrument; it is just something to prime your own idea pump. For example, say you want to write about the movie rating system. You could develop the following questionnaire for some students, faculty, family, and friends.

1. What do you think of the current movie rating system that uses the designations G, PG, PG-13, R, X, and NC-17?

2. Why do you think the way you do?

3. What could be done to improve the system?

4. What aspects of the current system should remain the same?

Your questionnaire should not include too many questions, or people will not bother with it. Nor should you use the answers *instead* of your own thinking; the answers are meant to help you develop your own ideas and perspective. Finally, question at least 10 people, so you get a useful number of responses.

WRITE AN EXPLORATORY DRAFT

Sometimes when you do not know what to write, the solution is to get in there and write anyway. You may be one of those people who don't know what they want to say until they say it. If so, sit down and force yourself to write on your topic for about an hour without worrying about how good the material is. The result will be an exploratory draft, a few pages of material reflecting what you currently know. An exploratory draft may yield a thought or two that you can pursue with one of the idea generation techniques in this chapter, or it may yield enough for you to try an outline or rough draft. Remember that your goal is not to produce a first draft of your essay; it is to discover one or more ideas to serve as a departure point.

RELATE THE TOPIC TO YOUR OWN EXPERIENCE

When you are assigned a topic, if ideas do not occur to you, try relating the topic to your own experiences. For example, if you have been asked to write about modern technology, remember all the trouble your used car has caused you, and write an essay about how cars can be more trouble than they are worth. Or recall all the times computer errors have caused you problems and write about the frustrations of the computer age. If you have been asked to write about the American educational system, think about your child-care hassles and argue that your college should have a day-care center. A topic that seems formidable at first can be made manageable if it is viewed in the context of your own life experiences.

TALK INTO A TAPE RECORDER

Forget writing for a while and try talking. Have a conversation with yourself about your topic by speaking all your thoughts into a tape recorder. Do not censor yourself; just talk about whatever occurs to you, and feel free to be silly, offbeat, funny, dramatic, or outlandish. When you run out of ideas, play back the tape. When you hear a good idea, pause the tape and write the idea down.

TALK TO OTHER PEOPLE

Discuss your writing topic with friends and relatives. They may be able to suggest ideas. Or have other people ask you questions about your topic. Your answers may include ideas to develop your topic. The brainstorming questions on page 24–25 can provide a starting point.

WRITE A POEM

Sometimes changing formats can help, so instead of trying to write an essay, write a poem about your topic. Then study it for ideas you can shape and develop in essay form.

WRITE ABOUT YOUR BLOCK

When all else fails, write about why you can't write. Explain how you feel, what is keeping you from getting ideas, and what you would write if you could. This sheer act of writing can catapult you beyond the block to productive idea generation.

PUT YOUR TOPIC ON THE BACK BURNER

If you do not know what to write, you may need to give your ideas an incubation period. Try going about your normal routine with your writing topic on the back burner. Think about your topic from time to time throughout the day. Many writers get some of their best ideas while walking the dog, washing the car, sitting in a traffic jam, cleaning the house, and such. If you feel anxious, exercise to relieve the tension. Of course, if an idea strikes while you are in the middle of something, stop and write the idea down so you do not forget it.

IDENTIFY YOUR WRITING CONTEXT

You may have trouble thinking of ideas if you have not clarified your purpose, audience, and role (the writing context; see page 6). Responding to the following can help.

1. **To identify your purpose:**

    a. What feelings, ideas, or experiences can I relate to my reader?

    b. Of what can I inform my reader?

    c. Of what can I persuade my reader?

    d. In what way can I entertain my reader?

2. **To identify your audience:**

    a. Who could learn something from my writing?

    b. Who would enjoy reading about my topic?

    c. Who could be influenced to think or act a certain way?

    d. Who is interested in my topic or would find it important?

    e. Who needs to hear what I have to say?

3. **If you have trouble establishing your role, try one of these:**

student	citizen	friend	child
employee	neutral party	authority	spouse
parent	average,	woman or man	voter
teenager	general reader	consumer	

KEEP A JOURNAL

Buy a full-size spiral notebook for keeping a journal, and write in it every day. A journal is not a diary because it is not a record of your daily activities. Instead, it is an account of your thoughts and reactions to events. For example, if you feel compassion for a blind person you saw, describe your feelings. If you are anxious about an upcoming event, explain why you are concerned. If you were recently reminded of a childhood event, describe this memory.

A journal is also a good place to think things through in writing. Is something troubling you? Do you have a problem? Explore the issues in your journal, and you may achieve new insights. In addition, if you are working on a writing project, a journal is an ideal place to try out an approach to part of the draft, or tinker with a revision. A journal is also an excellent place to respond to what goes on in your classes: Summarize class notes, respond to reading assignments, and react to lectures. Journal activities like these will help you learn course material.

Because your journal is meant for you and not for a reader, you do not need to revise and edit anything. Just get your ideas down any way that suits you because you are your primary audience this time. Later, if you are looking for a writing topic, review your journal for ideas.

The best way to handle journal writing is to set aside at least 15 minutes every day to write. If you have trouble thinking of what to write, try one of the following suggestions:

1. Write about something that angers you, that pleases you, or that frustrates you.

2. Describe the ideal college education.

3. Write about some change you would like to make in yourself

4. Look at a newspaper and respond to a headline.

5. Write about someone you admire.

6. Describe your life as you would like it to be in five years.

7. Tell about one thing the world could do without.

8. Record a vivid childhood memory.

9. Describe the best and worst features of your school.

10. Describe your current writing process, including what you do to generate ideas, draft, revise, and edit.

11. Describe one piece of legislation you wish you could draft. Explain how it would improve the world.

12. Record your reactions to your writing class so far: What do you find confusing? What has been helpful? What topics would you like to cover? What do you think of the pace of instruction?

COMBINE TECHNIQUES

You can combine techniques any way you like. Perhaps you will begin with freewriting and then try brainstorming. Or maybe you will talk into a tape recorder and then list. Experiment until you find the combination of techniques that works the best.

DEVELOP YOUR OWN WRITING TOPIC

If you must come up with your own writing topic, some of the following strategies may help.

1. Try freewriting (see page 20). Begin something like this: "I need a writing topic. Let's see, maybe I could write about . . ."

2. Try clustering (page 22). Begin by placing one of these subjects in a circle in the center of the page: education, athletics, friendship, television, movies, family, automobiles, teenagers, memories, technology, the environment.

3. Skim magazines and newspapers for ideas. An article on the Olympics could prompt you to write that the government should subsidize athletes.

4. Consult your journal for topic ideas (see page 28).

5. Fill in the blanks in the following sentences to arrive at possible writing topics:

   a. I'll never forget the time I _____.

   b. The best thing about _____ is _____.

   c. The worst thing about _____ is _____.

   d. My most embarrassing (or proudest) moment occurred when
      _____.

   e. I wish I could change _____.

   f. After _____ I changed my mind about _____.

   g. _____ is the most unforgettable person I know.

   h. _____ is the most _____ I know.

   i. The best way to _____ is _____.

j. Few people understand the true meaning of _____.

k. What this country needs is _____.

l. Without _____, life would be very different.

m. _____ made a lasting impression on me.

n. Few people understand the differences between _____ and _____.

o. _____ and _____ are more alike than people realize.

Filling in the blanks in these sentences will not give you ready-to-use topics, but the completed sentences will *suggest* topics. For example, consider this completed sentence:

I wish I could change the way public education is funded in this state.

This sentence could lead to the following topic:

Rather than using the property tax, this state should finance public education with an increased income tax.

6. Make a list of questions or problems, and use one of the questions or problems as a departure point for additional idea generation. For example, your list could include some of the following:

a. Do nice people really finish last?

b. What is the best way to find a job?

c. Why do women wear makeup when men don't?

d. How can I improve my conversation skills?

e. Is it too late to save our environment?

f. Why do so few people vote?

g. Why are violent movies so popular?

USE A COMPUTER

If you use a computer, you may like the following strategies.

Freewriting

A computer is great for freewriting. (See page 20 on freewriting.) With a blank screen, begin to write whatever comes to mind about your subject (or even your lack of a subject). Do not go back with the delete key, the backspace key, or the left arrow key. Just write for about five or ten minutes. Then get a printout, and read what you have typed. Underline usable ideas. Perhaps there will be enough to get you started. If not, do a second freewriting focusing on the underlined ideas.

Blindfolded Writing

No, you don't really blindfold yourself or even close your eyes. Just find the switch that controls the brightness of the monitor and turn it all the way down until the screen is dark. Then type for five to ten minutes, just as you would if you were freewriting. When you are done, your screen may look like this:

> I kdon;t know what to write I think I;ll write about the problems of students are getting wripped off on the fees and tuition being changerd.

That's not a problem. You can still detect the seeds of good ideas to expand on in a draft or in a second blindfolded writing.

Write E-Mail

Write an e-mail to a friend or classmate and discuss your writing topic. Mention the ideas you currently have and ask for a response to those ideas and for some additional ideas to consider.

Surf the Internet

Type your topic into a search engine and scan the titles returned. If you like, go to some of the more interesting sites and see where they lead.

Keep an Electronic Journal

Journaling can be done on a computer, just as well as in a spiral notebook. Create a journal file and write in it each day, according to the guidelines on page 28.

Listing and Writing a Scratch Outline

You may appreciate listing on the computer because ideas can be easily re-organized and deleted to get a neat, sequenced list of ideas.

To list at the computer, write the first idea that comes to mind. A word or a phrase will do just fine. Press the enter or return key. Write another idea, and press the enter or return key. Repeat these steps until you run out of ideas.

Use your delete key(s) to eliminate ideas you want to strike from your list. Next, study your list and decide what order is suggested. Try out the order using the copy-move sequence. Rearrange your list as often as you like until you have a suitable scratch outline to guide your first draft.

Cut and Paste

If you generate ideas on the computer, you can cut and paste some or all of that material into a first draft. Of course, you will need to revise that material later, but it may work well as a departure point.

2

"How Do I Write a Thesis?"

Knowing in your own mind what your essay is about is not enough. You need to convey that idea to your reader in a clear, appealing way—and that's where your *thesis* comes in. Your thesis is the statement of your essay's main point (see page 10), and it frequently appears in your opening paragraph—the *introduction* (see page 10). Because your thesis guides the course of your essay, it is very important and needs to be crafted with care. The suggestions in this chapter can help.

Study Your Idea Generation Material

It may be tempting to base your thesis on the point you generated the most ideas for, but that point may not be your best choice. Perhaps you have too much material for the length you are working with, or perhaps that point holds little interest for your reader. Study your idea generation material carefully with your reader in mind before deciding what point to shape into your thesis.

Write a Two-Part Thesis

One part of your thesis should give the topic you are discussing, and the other part should note your opinion about that topic. In the following examples, the topic is underlined once, and the opinion is underlined twice.

The television ratings system does not serve the purpose it was intended to serve.
The federal government should outlaw Internet gambling.
Although textbooks cost a great deal of money, they are one of the best bargains in education.
It is not fair that teachers get preferential parking on this campus.

NOTE THE MAIN POINTS THAT WILL BE MADE IN YOUR ESSAY

In addition to noting your topic and your opinion on that topic, your thesis can indicate the main points you will cover in your body paragraphs (although it does not have to do this). In the following example, the designated main points are underlined.

Year-round schools are a good idea because children would not forget material over long summer breaks, child care would not be a problem for working parents, and a greater number of elective courses could be offered.

LIMIT YOUR TOPIC TO SOMETHING MANAGEABLE

Avoid treating more than one topic or more than one opinion. Also avoid single topics that are too broad. Treating more than one topic, more than one opinion, or a very broad topic requires you to write too much, or it forces you into a very general, superficial treatment of your topic.

More than one topic:	To revitalize the city, tax incentives should be offered to new businesses, and more parking should be offered downtown.
Better (one topic):	To revitalize the city, tax incentives should be offered to new businesses.
Better (one topic):	To revitalize the city, more parking should be offered downtown.
More than one opinion:	Voters would be less apathetic if campaign finance laws were changed, and if candidates debated more often.
Better (one opinion):	Voters would be less apathetic if campaign finance laws were changed.
Better (one opinion):	Voters would be less apathetic if candidates debated more often.

Too broad: The American political system needs to be over-
hauled.

Better: The electoral college is no longer a sensible way to
elect a president.

Express Your Opinion in Specific Words

Words like *good, nice, awesome, bad,* and *interesting* are too vague to give
your reader a clear indication of your opinion, so opt instead for more specific words and phrases.

Vague: Jennifer Juarez makes a <u>good</u> candidate for City Council.

Better: Jennifer Juarez is a qualified candidate for City Council because of her
extensive political background.

Vague: New York's Metropolitan Museum is an <u>awesome</u> place.

Better: Because of the number and variety of its holdings, New York's
Metropolitan Museum is a national treasure.

Avoid Factual Statements

If your thesis is a statement of indisputable fact, your essay will have
nowhere to go.

Factual statement: The zoning board must decide whether to approve a housing development on Route 193.

Better: The zoning board should approve the housing development
on Route 193.

Avoid Announcing Your Intentions

Thesis statements that include wordings like "This essay will show," "In
the following paragraphs I will explain," and "My purpose is to demonstrate" are heavy-handed and best avoided.

Announcement: The purpose of this paper is to show why state lotteries are
harmful to the average person.

Better: State lotteries are harmful to the average person.

THINK OF YOUR THESIS AS TENTATIVE

During drafting and revision, everything is part of a process of discovery and, therefore, subject to change. Your thesis, no matter how carefully you crafted it, is tentative. It may change later, as new insights occur to you.

3

"How Do I Get My Ideas to Fit Together?"

Okay, so you've come up with good ideas and now you need an organizational framework to help your ideas hang together in a coherent whole. The strategies in this chapter can help you put that framework together.

Check Your Thesis

Your thesis tells what your essay is about. It can be written out (often appearing in the introduction) or strongly suggested by the details in the essay. For more on the thesis, see Chapter 2. If your ideas do not come together, the problem may be with your thesis. Check your thesis against the guidelines that follow and make any necessary adjustments.

1. **Be sure you have a thesis.** Can you point to or write out a specific sentence or two that expresses the focus of your writing? If not, your ideas may be merely a collection of loosely related thoughts that seem confused because they do not develop one central focus.

2. **Be sure your thesis expresses an idea worthy of discussion,** something that is disputed or something in need of explanation. For more on this point, see page 36.

3. **Be sure your thesis does not take in too much territory,** or you will be forced to bring in too many ideas, which can create disorder.

Thesis covering too
　　much territory:　High school was a traumatic experience for me.

Acceptable thesis:　My first high school track meet was a traumatic experience for me.

Explanation:　The first thesis requires the writer to cover events spanning four years—a great deal for one essay. The second thesis sets up a more reasonable goal—covering the events of one afternoon.

WRITE A SCRATCH OUTLINE

To write a scratch outline, list all your main points. Then review the list and number the points in the order you will handle them in your writing. A scratch outline can be made quickly, and many writers find it is all they need to get organized. However, because the outline is not very detailed (it covers only the main points), other writers find it does not provide enough structure. If you are one of the latter, you may prefer one of the other outlining techniques described in this chapter.

CONSTRUCT AN OUTLINE TREE

The outline tree provides a visual representation of how ideas relate to each other. To construct a tree, write your thesis on the page:

A refundable deposit should be added to the price of products in glass containers.

Next, branch your main ideas off from your thesis idea:

A refundable deposit should be added to the price of products in glass containers.

to reduce litter　because voluntary recycling is not working　to keep prices down

Then, branch supporting ideas off from your main ideas:

The value of the outline tree is that it allows you to see at a glance how ideas relate to each other so that when drafting, you avoid skipping randomly from one idea to another.

COMPLETE AN OUTLINE WORKSHEET

An outline worksheet allows you to plan your draft in a fair amount of detail without bothering with the roman numerals, letters, and numbers of a formal outline. To use the worksheet, make a copy of the form in Figure 1 and fill in the blanks with words and phrases that indicate the points you will make in the draft. Then write the draft using the worksheet as a guide.

MAKE OUTLINE CARDS

After generating ideas, write each of your ideas on its own index card, and then arrange the cards in the order you will treat the ideas in your draft. If this order does not work, rearrange the cards and try again.

Figure 1
OUTLINE WORKSHEET

Paragraph I
1. Opening comments to stimulate reader's interest: _____

_____

_____

2. Thesis statement: _____

_____

_____

Paragraph II
1. Main point (topic sentence idea): _____

_____

_____

2. Supporting details to develop main point: _____

_____

_____

Paragraph III
1. Main point (topic sentence idea): _____

_____

_____

2. Supporting details to develop main point: _____

_____

_____

_____

Note: Continue in this way until all main points are treated.

Final paragraph
Ideas to bring writing to closure: _____

_____

_____

_____

CONSTRUCT AN OUTLINE MAP

An outline map is a good way to plan a draft and get a visual representation of it. To develop the map, use your list of generated ideas to fill in a copy of the form shown in Figure 2.

To complete the map, write in your thesis and place one main point at the top of each column. (If you have two main points, you will have two columns; three main points will mean three columns, and so on.) In the columns under each main point, write the supporting ideas that will develop the main point. Then note what your concluding point(s) will be.

The beauty of the outline map is that before you begin drafting you can check the relevance of ideas by checking what is in each column against the main point at the top, and you can check the relevance of each main point by comparing it to the thesis. Also, if ideas need to be added or moved around, you can do so relatively easily.

You can write your draft from the map by allowing each column to be a body paragraph, with each main point expressed in a topic sentence.

WRITE AN ABSTRACT

An *abstract* is a very brief summary. Before you draft, write a one-paragraph abstract of what you plan to say in your writing. Include only the main points, and leave out the details that will expand on those points. Then read over your abstract to check that the main points follow logically one to the next. If they do not, try another abstract, placing your ideas in a different order. When you draft, you can flesh out the abstract into a full-length piece of writing.

USE A COMPUTER

Computers can be very handy for helping writers organize their ideas. Try some of the techniques that follow even if you do not usually compose at the computer.

The Scratch Outline

If you use a computer to generate ideas by listing, your list can be turned into a scratch outline very easily. Using the delete key, eliminate the ideas in your list that you do not want to use (and if new ideas occur to you, add them to the list). Then using the copy-paste command, arrange the ideas in the order you want to treat them in your writing.

Figure 2
OUTLINE MAP

Thesis: _____				
_____				
Main Point (Topic Sentence Idea)	Main Point (Topic Sentence Idea)	Main Point (Topic Sentence Idea)	Main Point (Topic Sentence Idea)
Supporting Detail	Supporting Detail	Supporting Detail	Supporting Detail

Concluding points: _____
_____
_____
_____
_____

The Outline Program

If an outline program is available to you, use it to fill in the various levels
designated by roman numerals, letters, and numbers. Study the results and
expand and delete sublevels as necessary.

Create Your Own Outline File

If your word processing program does not include an outline feature, develop your own outline form, using roman numerals, letters, and numbers.
Save the form as a file you can retrieve whenever you want to outline. You
can also create forms and files for the outline map and outline worksheet.

II

DRAFTING

Drafting *is your first attempt to get your ideas down on the page. Because drafting occurs so early in the writing process, the draft is likely to be very rough. This is normal, so do not feel discouraged if your draft needs considerable work.*

4

"I Know What I Want to Say, but I Can't Say It."

Okay, so you think you know what you want to say, and you sit down with plenty of fresh writing paper, pencils sharpened to a lethal point, and a bowl of Doritos. Then disaster strikes: You know what you want to say, but the words don't come out right—or they don't come out at all. If this happens to you, be assured that you are not alone. Plenty of writers experience this kind of block. The key to getting past the block to productive writing rests in the techniques described in this chapter.

Get Rid of Distractions

Are you trying to write with headphones on? With TV on in the background? With your roommate rummaging around looking for a missing left sneaker? With the street department outside tearing up the pavement with an air hammer? Few people can write when distractions disrupt their focus, so getting past writer's block may be as simple as finding a place to write that is free of distractions.

Set Intermediate Goals for Yourself

At the beginning of a writing project, the finish line can seem so far away that we feel stress. This stress can lead to writer's block. In this case, the key to getting unstuck is to break the task down into manageable steps, so the completion of each step is a goal that earns its own reward. For example, the first time you sit down, tell yourself you will just come up with five ideas and a scratch outline. The second time, you will just write the draft of the introduction. The third time, you will draft two more paragraphs. If you work toward the completion of intermediate goals, the project will be less intimidating.

ALLOW YOUR DRAFT TO BE ROUGH

If you find yourself starting a draft, crumpling up the paper and pitching it to the floor, starting another draft, crumpling up the paper and pitching it to the floor, starting another draft and so forth, you may be expecting too much too soon. Remember, a first draft is supposed to be rough. Instead of wadding up that draft, force yourself to go from start to finish in one sitting to get raw material to shape during the revision process that comes later.

WRITE IN A NEW PLACE

A change of scene can help a writer break through a block, so if you usually write in one place, try another. Go to the library, the park, or a local diner. If you write in your room, try the lounge or a classroom, or the dining hall. A new locale can give you a fresh perspective.

SWITCH YOUR WRITING TOOLS

If you write with a pen, try a pencil or a computer. If you use a computer, try a pen. If you like lined paper, try unlined. If you like legal pads, try stationery. Do anything to make the writing *feel* different, and you may break through the block.

WRITE ON A DAILY SCHEDULE

Professional writers are usually very disciplined about their work. They make themselves sit down at the same time each day to write for a specific number of hours. You can follow the lead of the professionals and push past the block by forcing yourself to write at a certain time each day for a specific length of time.

WRITE A LETTER TO A FRIEND

Sometimes we think of the reader at the other end sitting in judgment of our work, and we freeze. To relax and break the block, write your draft as if it were a letter to a friend—a letter to someone who cares about you and who will value you regardless of how well you write. When your audience is shifted to a person you feel comfortable with, you can relax and allow the words to emerge. After writing a draft this way, you will have to revise your work to make it suitable for your intended reader and to shape it into essay or other appropriate form, but you should have considerable raw material to work with.

WRITE FOR YOURSELF INSTEAD OF FOR A READER

Some writers block because they imagine the reader passing judgment, and they become tense. One good solution is to forget your reader for a while and write the draft in a way that pleases *you*. Be your own audience at first. Later when you polish your work, you can make the changes necessary for the audience you are aiming for.

WRITE IN A NATURAL STYLE

Sometimes writers try so hard to achieve what they think is a "college" style that the strain causes a block. To solve this problem, write as you normally speak, and the words should flow more easily. After drafting this way, revise if the writing is too conversational or informal.

Unnatural: The garrulous male juvenile who, upon cursory examination gave the appearance of being about 12, nettled the orator.

More natural: The talkative boy, who looked about 12, annoyed the speaker.

SPEAK INTO A TAPE RECORDER

A variation of the previous technique is to speak your draft into a tape recorder. Sometimes we have trouble writing, but we do not have trouble talking. After speaking into a tape recorder, you can transcribe the tape to get your draft.

REREAD OFTEN

If you get stuck, go back and reread your draft from the beginning. Doing so can give you momentum and propel you past the block. Even when you are not blocked, frequent rereading can be a helpful reminder of your thesis, purpose, and organizational strategy, a reminder that keeps you on track.

WALK AWAY

When the words won't come, you may need time away to relax and let things simmer. Take a walk, listen to music, play tennis, take a shower, make a sandwich, read a magazine, clean a drawer, or pot a plant. Do anything to clear your mind for a while. Time away can serve as an incubation period, so when you start to write again you are no longer stuck.

WRITE THE INTRODUCTION LAST

If you cannot get the introduction down, write the rest of your essay and then go back to it. With the rest of your draft complete, you may find your introduction easier to handle than it was before. (If you write your introduction last, write a preliminary thesis on scratch paper so you have a focus for your draft.)

BEGIN IN THE MIDDLE

Begin writing whatever point you feel confident writing and go from there. Starting with an idea you can write—no matter where in the draft it falls—can propel you forward.

CONCENTRATE ON WHAT YOU *CAN* DO AND SKIP WHAT YOU CAN'T DO

A writer can start out just fine, but along the way begin to struggle and eventually come to a full stop. Why does a good start fizzle? Typically this happens because the writer dwells on the trouble spots and loses momentum. To solve this problem, just skip the trouble spots: If you cannot think of the right word, leave a blank and add it later; if you sense some detail is not working, underline it for later consideration and press on; if the right approach to your introduction escapes you, begin with your second paragraph and go on from there. By focusing on what you *can* do and leaving the problems behind to deal with later, you will make more progress.

RESIST THE TEMPTATION TO REWRITE AS YOU DRAFT

If you constantly rewrite what you have already written, you can get stuck in one place—maybe polishing the introduction over and over, or perhaps tinkering endlessly with the detail to support your first point. While some writers do well if they revise as they go, others get bogged down this way. As a result, getting to the finish line takes too long, and frustration sets in. When you draft, try pushing forward even if what you have already written is in pretty sorry shape. Later you can revise the rough spots.

WRITE FAST AND DON'T LOOK BACK

If you write fast, you will have no time to worry about how well you are saying things. You will only be able to get things down the best way you can at the moment. If you don't look back, you won't be tempted to rewrite anything. So write fast, don't look back, and you may be able to push past the block. Later when you revise, you can rework things as needed.

WRITE AN OUTLINE

If you have generated a number of good ideas and you still have trouble writing a draft, the problem may be that you are unsure what idea you should write first, second, third, and so on. An outline can be a great help here. For information on outlining, consult Chapter 3.

RETURN TO IDEA GENERATION

You may *not* have a clear enough idea of what you want to say, so you need to return to idea generation. Try a favorite technique to clarify your thinking or to flesh out some existing ideas. Or try a technique you have not used before (see Chapter 1 for suggestions).

THINK POSITIVELY

Positive thinkers outperform negative thinkers. Adopt a positive attitude by thinking of yourself as a writer, as someone who *can and will* get a draft down and revise it successfully.

USE A COMPUTER

If you like to compose at the computer, the next techniques may prove helpful.

Split Your Screen

On one part of the screen, display your outline or idea generation material; on the other side, display your draft. This way, you can readily refer to your prewriting material as you write. You can also place your thesis in one of the screens to help you stay on track as you draft.

Write Invisible Notes

Many word processing programs allow you to write notes that appear on your screen but not on the printed page. If you want to remember a question, record an idea, or make a comment for later consideration, and you do not want to interrupt your drafting, use this capability to write on your draft. The comments will not appear on your paper copy, but they will be saved for you to come back to.

5

"I'M HAVING TROUBLE WITH MY INTRODUCTION."

The first day of school, the first day on a new job, a first date—starting out is often hard. Starting out a piece of writing can also be difficult, even if you have generated plenty of ideas. The following strategies can help.

EXPLAIN WHY YOUR TOPIC IS IMPORTANT

Just why should your readers take time to read your essay? By explaining why your topic is important, you can engage their interest. For example, say you are writing to convince your readers of the importance of gender-neutral language. Your introduction could explain that such language affects people's view of the world:

> Some people say that the language we use reflects the world we live in. More often, our words help shape that world. For example, children who hear doctors repeatedly referred to as "he" may not realize that females can be doctors just as well as males. The public, accustomed to hearing "chairman of the board" rather than "chair" or "chairperson," may find female business executives somehow in violation of the natural order of things. Thus, gender-neutral language <u>does</u> matter because it helps create a world where people of both sexes can achieve their potential.

PROVIDE BACKGROUND INFORMATION

What must your reader know to appreciate or understand your topic? What information would establish a context for your essay? The answers to these questions can provide background information in the introduction. Assume you will argue that more federal money should be spent to educate children about the dangers of tobacco. Your introduction could supply background information about past efforts in this area.

> In the late 1990s President Clinton began an initiative to reduce tobacco use by children. The public was invited to comment, public officials made grand speeches, the press covered the proceedings extensively, and the result was a few Food and Drug Administration efforts to reduce access and limit the appeal of tobacco products for children. Basically, all this amounted to was some billboards and public service announcements on television. The effects have been minimal, and the public health crisis is worsening as children start smoking at younger ages. Clearly, the federal government must devote considerably more money and resources to educating children about tobacco.

TELL A STORY

Create interest in your topic by telling a story that is related to that topic or that in some way illustrates your thesis. For example, if your essay shows that modern conveniences can be more trouble than they are worth, the following introduction with a story could be effective:

> The morning of my job interview, I woke up an hour earlier than usual and took special pains with my hair and makeup. I ate a light, sensible breakfast which managed to hit bottom despite the menagerie of winged insects fluttering around my stomach. I drove the parkway downtown, nervously biting my lower lip the whole way. I had to park three long blocks from the office building where the interview was to take place, and by the time I got to the building I was completely windblown. Breathless, I gasped my name to the receptionist, who explained that my interview would have to be postponed. The personnel director had never made it in. It seems her electricity was off, and she could not get her car out of the garage because the door was controlled by an electric opener. That's when I knew for sure that modern conveniences can be downright inconvenient.

USE AN INTERESTING QUOTATION

If someone has said something applicable to your thesis and said it particularly well, you can engage interest by quoting the remark. Just be sure that the quotation is interesting and not an overused expression like "better safe than sorry" or "the early bird gets the worm."

> Everyone seems to agree that we learn from our mistakes and that failure can be more instructive than success. As General Colin Powell has said, "There are no secrets to success. It is the result of preparation, hard work, learning from failure." Why, then, are students denied the opportunity to repeat courses without penalty? So we can profit from our mistakes, the administration should allow us to take courses three times and record the highest grade on our transcripts.

PROVIDE RELEVANT STATISTICS

Relevant statistics, particularly if they are surprising, can engage a reader. Just be sure that you note the source of the statistics you use, so your reader does not think you pulled them from the air.

> According to our campus newspaper, this college has spent $25 million for campus renovations in the last five years. During the same period, enrollment has dropped by 2,273 students, and 112 fewer people are employed here. These figures suggest that the administration cares more about buildings than people. It is time to reverse the trend and work to increase enrollment, faculty, and staff.

FIND SOME COMMON GROUND WITH YOUR READER

Finding common ground with your reader involves identifying a point of view or experience you and your reader share. Presenting this common ground in an introduction can create a bond between reader and writer. In the following introduction, the common ground is a shared school experience:

> Think back to when you were in high school. Remember the kids who caused all the trouble, the ones who disrupted the teacher and made it difficult for the rest of the class to learn? They were the students who did not want to be in school anyway and made things miserable for the students who did want to be there. Now imagine how much more learning would have oc-

curred if the troublemakers had been allowed to quit school and get jobs. If we abolish compulsory attendance, everyone will be better off.

DESCRIBE SOMETHING

Because description adds interest and liveliness to writing, describing something can be an excellent way to begin:

> At 5 feet 3 inches and 170 pounds, Mr. Daria looked like a meatball. His stringy black hair, always in need of a cut, kept sliding into his eyes, and his too-tight shirts would not stay tucked into his too-tight polyester pants. He wore the same sport coat everyday; it was easily identified by the grease splotch on the left lapel. Yes, Mr. Daria was considered a nerd by most of the student body, but to me he was the best history teacher on the planet.

BEGIN WITH THE THESIS AND THE POINTS YOU WILL DISCUSS

Sometimes the direct approach is the best. You can begin by stating your thesis and the main points you will discuss, like this:

> Carolyn Hotimsky is the best candidate for mayor for two reasons. First, as president of city council, she demonstrated leadership ability. Second, as chief investment counselor for First City Bank, she learned about sound fiscal management.

KEEP IT SHORT

If you are having trouble with something, it makes no sense to make it as long as possible. Thus, if your introduction is proving troublesome, just write your thesis and one or two other sentences, and get on with the rest of your writing. If all else fails, just write your thesis and go on to your first point to be developed.

WRITE IT LAST

If you cannot come up with a suitable introduction, go on to write the rest of your piece and then return to the introduction. With the rest of your writing drafted, you may find that an approach to your introduction comes to mind. However, if you skip your introduction, jot down a working thesis on scratch paper and check it periodically to be sure you do not stray off into unrelated areas.

USE A COMPUTER

If you use a computer, you may like the following techniques.

Windowing. If you cannot decide which of two or more approaches to use, execute the command that lets you divide your screen in half. Then try one approach to your introduction in one-half of the screen and another approach in the other half. Compare the two approaches and decide which works better.

Turn Your Conclusion into the Introduction. It may sound strange, but your last paragraph may work better as an introduction than as a conclusion. To find out, execute the command that allows you to move your conclusion to the beginning of your writing. With some fine-tuning, you may be able to turn the conclusion into a strong introduction. Of course, you will have to write a new conclusion, but that may prove easier than wrestling with the introduction.

6

"How Do I Back Up What I Say?"

You may be a warm, wonderful human being and as honest as they come, but no experienced reader will believe what you say unless you back up your statements with proof and explanations. The suggestions in this chapter can help you with this.

Examine Your Own Experience

Convincing evidence can be drawn from your own life experiences. Say, for example, that you are discussing problems created by computers, and you wish to make the point that rather than improve efficiency, computers often contribute to procrastination. You might write a paragraph like the following, based on your own experience.

> Computers can be great time-wasters. The last time I sat down to write a paper, I found myself playing solitaire instead of drafting. The next thing I knew, an hour had gone by. I got myself back on task, but when I became stuck, I decided to check my e-mail. By the time I read and responded to five messages, another 20 minutes was lost. I tried to work on my paper again, but I was lured away by my favorite chatroom. I couldn't believe it when the clock in the corner of my screen showed that I had spent an hour discussing the latest Sheryl Crow CD. When I realized how much time I had wasted, I went straight back to my paper, but I was so tired that I know I didn't give it my best efforts. I probably would have done better had I used a pen and paper.

CONSIDER WHAT YOU OBSERVE

Excellent support for ideas can come from your observations of the world. Say you are discussing the trend to require volunteerism in high schools. Your observation of the kind of volunteer work students do at local high schools could lead to this paragraph.

Students can learn a great deal when they are required to perform volunteer service. However, care must be taken with the kinds of activities they are allowed to engage in. At our local high school, students were at first involved in such worthy activities as volunteering in hospitals, purchasing groceries for elderly neighbors, and coaching youth soccer. Now they receive volunteer credit for such dubious activities as helping out in the school office during study hall, working on theater sets for the senior play, and selling programs at football games. I doubt very much is learned from such work.

TELL A STORY

Search your own experience for brief stories that can drive home your points. Consider this passage, for example:

Distance running is an excellent sport for adolescents because even if they do not finish near the front of the pack, they can still feel good about themselves. Shaving a few seconds off an earlier time or completing a difficult course can be a genuine source of pride for a young runner.

Now notice how the addition of a brief story helps prove the point:

Distance running is an excellent sport for adolescents because even if they do not finish near the front of the pack, they can still feel good about themselves. Shaving a few seconds off an earlier time or completing a difficult course can be a genuine source of pride for a young runner. I remember a race I ran as a sophomore. I was recovering from a miserable cold and not in peak condition. Just after completing the first mile, I developed a cramp in my side. However, I was determined to finish, no matter how long it took me. Quarter mile by quarter mile, I ran rather haltingly. My chest was tight from lack of training because I had been sick, and my side hurt, but still I kept on. Eventually, I crossed the finish line, well back in the standings. However, I could not have been more proud of myself if I had won. I showed that I had what it took to finish, even though the going was tough.

DESCRIBE PEOPLE AND PLACES

Description allows you to create vivid images that help the reader to see and hear the way you see and hear. It also adds interest and vitality to writing. Consider this passage, for example:

> The best teacher I ever had was Mrs. Suarez, who taught me algebra in the ninth grade. But even more than teaching me algebra, Mrs. Suarez showed me compassion during a very difficult time in my life. I will always be grateful for her understanding and encouragement when I needed them most.
> In the ninth grade, I was a troubled teen, a victim of a difficult home life. Somehow Mrs. Suarez recognized my pain and approached me one day. . . .

Now notice the interest created with the addition of description:

> The best teacher I ever had was Mrs. Suarez, who taught me algebra in the ninth grade. But even more than teaching me algebra, Mrs. Suarez showed me compassion during a very difficult time in my life. To look at this woman, a person would never guess what a caring nature she had. With wire-stiff hair teased and lacquered into a bouffant, Mrs. Suarez looked like a hard woman. Her face, heavily wrinkled, had a scary, witchlike quality that befit the shrill voice she used to reprimand 14-year-old sinners who neglected their homework. She always stood ramrod straight with her 120 pounds evenly distributed over her orthopedic shoes. Many a freshman has been frightened by a first look at this no-nonsense woman. However, appearances are, indeed, deceptive, for Mrs. Suarez was not the witch she looked to be. In fact, I will always be grateful for her understanding and encouragement when I needed them most.

PROVIDE EXAMPLES

Nothing clarifies matters like a well-chosen example, so examples are an excellent way to back up what you say. Examples can come from personal experience, observation, reading and research, or classroom experience. Assume, for example, that you have stated that television commercials cause us to buy products and services we do not need. You could back up that point with examples you have observed, like this:

> Television commercials often make people want products they do not need. For example, Tony the Tiger urges children to eat highly sugared cereal, while gorgeous, bikini-clad women romp on the beach, luring men to

consume beer. Before Christmas, expensive toys based on the latest action hero are advertised relentlessly, until children are convinced they cannot survive without them. Of course, the worst offenders are the advertisers of hair dye, mascara, lipstick, perfume, and teeth-whiteners, who convince women they cannot be attractive without a drawer full of these products.

You could also take an example from personal experience (the time you went to a tax preparer because a commercial wrongly convinced you that you could not do your own taxes); you could draw an example from research (talk to others about unnecessary products they have purchased as a result of commercials); or you could cite an example you learned in the classroom (perhaps statistics on the number of people who buy a particular unnecessary product).

GIVE REASONS

Reasons help prove that something is true. Let's say that your point is that final examinations should be eliminated. These reasons could help prove your point: Finals create too much anxiety; they do not really show what a student knows; it is not fair to place considerable emphasis on one examination; some students test poorly. Here is how those reasons might appear in a paragraph:

Final examinations should be eliminated because they are not a sound educational practice. For one thing, these exams create too much anxiety among students. They worry so much about their performance that they lose sleep, stop eating, and show other signs of stress. Certainly, they cannot demonstrate what they know under such circumstances. They also cannot show what they really know because the tests cannot test all of a body of knowledge—just what the teacher wants to test. As a result, some of what a student knows may never be asked for. Furthermore, if the test is poorly constructed (and many of them are), students may further be kept from demonstrating their real learning. Then there is the fact that many students are poor test-takers. They may know the material just fine but be incapable of demonstrating their knowledge because they have never mastered the art of test-taking.

SHOW SIMILARITIES OR DIFFERENCES

Assume you are writing about ways to improve the quality life in nursing homes, and you make the point that nursing homes should allow residents to have pets. The following paragraph shows how you can back up your point by citing similarities.

Because nursing homes have long recognized the value of having young children visit residents, preschool classes are often invited to spend time in the facilities. Allowing the residents to have pets would be similarly beneficial. Just as the children do, the pets would provide companionship for the residents and give them an opportunity to express affection. Also, just as it does with children, the interaction with pets would provide intellectual stimulation and an opportunity to forget about infirmities. Of course, in one respect, pets are better than children: they do not have to go home at the end of the day because they already are home and can continue to make life better for residents.

Now assume that you want to argue that having pets in nursing homes is not a good idea. Showing differences can help you back up your point.

Some people claim that having pets in nursing homes would be beneficial in the same way that having preschoolers there is beneficial. This is not true. First, children will not add cost to a nursing home or its residents. Their parents feed them and take care of medical expenses, but the residents or nursing home would have to assume these expenses for pets. Also, because children are supervised by their teachers while in the facility, residents need not watch them very closely. Pets, on the other hand, need to be restrained from entering the rooms of residents who do not want to be near them. Since many residents cannot supervise the animals all the time, an already overburdened staff would have even more responsibility. Finally, children go home at the end of the day, but pets stay and require ongoing care, which can drain nursing home resources.

EXPLAIN CAUSES OR EFFECTS

If you are writing about sex education in schools and make the point that it should be mandatory, you can back up this point by citing the positive effects of sex education, like this:

Sex education's most obvious benefit is increased knowledge. Since it is unlikely that sexually active teens will start to abstain, increased knowledge about birth control will prevent unwanted pregnancy. Furthermore, the same knowledge can help teens protect themselves against sexually transmitted disease. When fewer teens become pregnant, more of them will stay in school and thus will not fall victim to unemployment, drugs, and crime. When more teens protect themselves against sexually transmitted diseases, fewer will die.

If you want to emphasize the need for sex education by citing the pressure on teenagers to become sexually active, you might explain what causes teenagers to become sexually active, like this:

> One reason teenagers are sexually active at a younger age is that they are bombarded by sexual messages. On MTV, videos are populated with women wearing next to nothing; men and women are touching, groping, and grinding in sexually provocative ways. On the radio, rock lyrics glorify teen sex as healthy rebellion and a sign of independence. Movies, too, send sexual messages. Sex scenes and nudity are frequent in PG-13 movies and are standard fare in R-rated movies that teens get into with no trouble at all. Much of the sex and nudity are unnecessary. For example, <u>Doc Hollywood</u>, rated PG-13, has a lengthy scene of a woman bathing nude in a lake. Nothing would have been lost if the woman had been swimming in the lake instead—with her bathing suit on.

To discover causes, ask yourself, "Why does this happen?" The answers may provide your details. Similarly, to discover effects, ask yourself, "After this happens, then what?" The answers may provide details as well. For example, ask, "Why do teenagers engage in sex?" and you might get the answer, "To be more like an adult." The desire to be mature then becomes a cause. Ask yourself, "After sex education courses are offered, then what?" If you get the answer, "Teenagers learn safe sex practices," you have an effect of sex education.

EXPLAIN HOW SOMETHING IS MADE OR DONE

Assume you are discussing simple things people can do to combat prejudice. If you make the point that people do not have to put up with racial, ethnic, or sexist humor, you might back up that point by explaining how a person can deal with such humor, like this:

> Many people do not know how to respond when they are told a racial, ethnic, or sexist joke, so they smile or laugh politely, even though they feel uncomfortable. A better approach is to say something simple, such as, "I don't find such jokes funny." Then, you can quickly turn the conversation to some neutral topic. If the joke was told to several people, and you do not want to embarrass the speaker, draw him or her aside later and say, "I'm sure you did not mean to, but you made me very uncomfortable when you told your joke." Both of these approaches let the speaker know that hurtful jokes are not universally welcome.

Explain What Would Happen if Your View Were Not Adopted

Say, for example that you are arguing for the passage of a tax levy to fund the building of a new high school. To help make your point, you can explain what would happen if the levy did *not* pass, like this:

Without the passage of the levy, funds would not be available to finance a new high school. Yet without the high school, our children will suffer. The current building is too small, and enrollment is projected to increase over the next five years. Thus, classes will be seriously overcrowded. Furthermore, the current building lacks an auditorium, making it impossible to have a theater program. The lack of an auditorium also means assemblies and band concerts must be held in the gym, where the acoustics are poor and the seats are uncomfortable. Most worrisome is the fact that the renovations required in the existing building, including asbestos removal, a new roof, and updated heating system, will cost almost as much as building a new school. If we spend money on these renovations, the children will reap no benefits, the way they would with a new building.

Consider the Opposition

If you are arguing a point, think about the view of those who disagree with you. If they have a compelling point, you can acknowledge it and offer your counterargument. For example, if you were arguing in favor of warning labels on CDs and tapes with sexually explicit lyrics, you could write the following.

People against warning labels cite the "forbidden fruit" argument. They say that young people will be encouraged to buy music with the labels, expressly because they are being warned away from them. To some extent this is true. However, the labels will still provide a guideline for parents who want to buy music for their children. They will also create an atmosphere of acceptability. Although young people may ignore them, the labels still send a message that some things are more appropriate than others for teenagers. This atmosphere is an improvement over the current "anything goes" climate that sends the message that teens can buy and do whatever they please. Down the road, stores may even refuse to sell labeled music to those under 21.

USE MATERIAL FROM OUTSIDE SOURCES

Statistics, facts, quotations, and ideas from outside sources can provide important support for many topics. These sources can include your textbooks and class lectures, newspapers, magazines, and sources you discover in the library or on the Internet. You should judge the credibility of any material from outside sources by assessing the following:

- **The author's credentials.** Check book jackets, headnotes, and biographies to learn about the author's current position, publications, degrees, affiliations, and such. They can suggest how knowledgeable he or she is on the subject. If necessary, consult a biographical dictionary in your library's reference room. Also, be wary of authors with an obvious bias because they will not offer objective information.

- **The timeliness of the piece.** For some subjects, you must have the most current information, so an article written 10 years ago will not be satisfactory.

- **The reliability of a website.** Many websites offer accurate, up-to-date information, but others are not very reliable. Evaluating a website is not always easy, so be skeptical. How does the site look? If it is amateurish, if there are misspellings, if it lacks links to substantial sites, it may not be reliable. Check who sponsors the site. Is it a known organization, like National Geographic, or an unknown source, lacking credentials? Many sites note the last update. A recent update suggests credibility.

Be warned: Avoid sites that offer student papers. The papers are not very good, so they will not earn you a respectable grade. In fact, they most likely will earn you an F for plagiarism (academic dishonesty).

CHAPTER

7

"I Don't Know How to End."

Imagine this: You go to the movies and pay $8.00 to see the latest action film. The beginning is wonderful—you're on the edge of your seat; the middle is very exciting—you're completely caught up in the plot. Then the ending comes—and it's awful. When you walk out of the theater, you probably do not talk about how good the beginning and middle were. Instead, you probably complain about how bad the ending was. Why? Because endings are important. They form the last impression, the one that is most remembered.

Your conclusion forms your reader's final impression If you write a weak conclusion, no matter how strong the rest of your piece is, your reader will feel let down. If you have trouble ending your writing, consult the strategies in this chapter.

Explain the Significance of Your Main Point

Anything appearing in the conclusion is emphasized because of its placement at the end, where it is most likely to be remembered. Therefore, the conclusion can be the best place for indicating the significance of your point. For example, let's say your essay told the story of the time you were cut from the junior high school basketball team. Your conclusion can explain the significance of the event, like this:

> Because being cut from the team shattered my self-esteem at such a young age, I have struggled all my life with feelings of inadequacy. I have doubted

my ability because the coach, whose judgment I trusted, told me that I didn't have what it takes.

PROVIDE A SUMMARY IF YOUR READER WILL APPRECIATE ONE

Summarizing your main points is a service to your reader if you have written a long piece or one with complex ideas. After reading a long or complicated writing, a reader will appreciate a review of the high points at the end. However, if your piece is short or if the ideas are easily grasped, your reader may find a summary a boring rehash of previously covered material.

EXPLAIN THE CONSEQUENCES OF IGNORING YOUR VIEW

If you are writing to persuade your reader to think or act a certain way, you can close effectively by explaining what would happen if your reader did not follow your recommendation. Assume, for example, that you are writing to convince your reader that a drug education program should be instituted in the local elementary school. After giving your reasons for this view, you could close like this:

> If we do not have a drug education program in the earliest grades, we miss the opportunity to influence our children when they are the most impressionable. If we miss this opportunity to influence them when they are young and responsive to adult pressure, we run the risk of losing our children to powerful peer pressure to experiment with drugs.

CONCLUDE WITH A POINT YOU WANT TO EMPHASIZE

Anything placed at the end is emphasized. Therefore, you can conclude with your most important point, the one you want underscored in your reader's mind. For example, if you are explaining the differences between child-rearing practices of today and those of 50 years ago, you could end like this:

> The most telling difference between child-rearing practices of today and those of 50 years ago is that today's parents are less rigid. Unlike the parents of 50 years ago, they are less concerned with doing everything on schedule and by the book. Babies are not forced to eat and sleep at specific times but may do so when they are hungry and sleepy. Today's parents trust their instincts more than they trust the child-care book used by parents of the

past. Thus, they are more likely to do what they think is right and not worry about what the "authorities" say.

RESTATE YOUR THESIS FOR EMPHASIS

Repetition can be effective if it provides emphasis, but repetition can be boring and annoying if the emphasis is uncalled for. Thus, if you decide to close by restating your thesis, be sure the restatement is effective emphasis rather than boring repetition. Also, avoid restating in the same language you used previously. Restate the thesis a *new* way.

SUGGEST A COURSE OF ACTION

If something can be done to remedy a problem your essay discusses, or if you can call your reader to action, do so in the conclusion. For example, if your essay explains the reason for declining enrollment at your school, you can suggest a course of action in the conclusion, like this:

> The reasons for our declining enrollment are complex, but the solution to the problem is clear. First, we should hire a recruitment specialist and charge that person with aggressively seeking new students. At the same time, we should begin a marketing campaign, complete with local television and radio spots, to attract area people so they attend school here rather than out of state. Finally, we should hire a marketing firm to discover what potential students are seeking and try to meet those desires. Yes, these measures are expensive, but the money will be well spent if we can return enrollment figures to their previous high levels.

ASK A QUESTION

You can leave your reader thinking about your point of view if you close with a suitable question, as exemplified in this conclusion for an essay about the wisdom of raising the speed limit on state routes.

> If the speed limit is raised, truckers would save money, as would those who ship their goods on trucks. And while studies do not support the contention that the higher speed limit will mean more accidents, they suggest that the accidents that do occur would involve more fatalities. Do we really want to save money but lose lives?

Look to the Future

Sometimes you can write an effective conclusion by looking ahead to the time beyond your essay. For example, say you have been explaining the benefits and drawbacks of purchasing goods on the Internet. You could close by looking to the future, like this:

> In a few short years, e-commerce will rival the popularity of traditional stores. New sites will allow us to comparison shop and take advantage of retailers that are not located where we live. We will be able to choose from a greater variety than many of us—especially those who live in small towns—now have. Because overhead is so low, prices are likely to be better than at the mall, even when shipping costs are factored in. Clearly, e-commerce will change the shopping experience even more dramatically than it already has.

Combine Approaches

You can combine any two or more approaches to create a strong conclusion. For example, you can summarize main points and then make a recommendation, or you can restate your thesis and then ask a question.

Keep It Short

If you have trouble with your conclusion, keep it short. You do not want to end abruptly, but you also should not take something that is a problem and stretch it out longer than necessary. A perfectly acceptable conclusion can be only one or two sentences.

CHAPTER

8

"I Can't Think of the Right Word."

You're writing along, and just as your confidence begins to surge—wham! Suddenly, you're stuck because you can't think of the right word. You try all the usual techniques—chewing on the end of your pencil to squeeze the word into the tip, rubbing your forehead to massage the word into your brain, and staring at the computer screen to will the word to appear—but nothing helps. Soon it's a matter of pride, and you refuse to budge until you think of the word that's lurking annoyingly just at the tip of your tongue. The next thing you know, 15 minutes have passed, you have made no progress, and you are frustrated.

When the word you need escapes you, avoid becoming frustrated and stalled by trying the techniques described in this chapter.

WRITE IN A NATURAL STYLE

You may have trouble finding the right word if you are writing in an unnatural style. Instead of writing with your own normal vocabulary, you may be straining for an overly "sophisticated" style, a style you think will impress the reader. As a result, words escape you because you are seeking ones that were never a natural part of your vocabulary in the first place. Return to a more natural style, and words should come more easily.

Unnatural: Attempting to ruminate her morning nourishment while simultaneously communicating the events that transpired, Emma began to choke on her victuals.

More natural: Trying to tell what happened at the same time she was eating breakfast, Emma began to choke.

69

Use ITTS

ITTS stands for "*I'm trying to say.*" When you cannot find the right word, stop for a moment and say to yourself, "I'm trying to say _____ ." Imagine yourself explaining what you mean to a friend and fill in the blank with the word or words you would speak to that friend. Then write the word or words in your draft. You may use several words or even a sentence to fill in the blank when originally you were only seeking a single word. That's fine.

Substitute a Phrase or a Sentence for a Troublesome Word

If you cannot take one path, then take an alternate route to your destination: If you cannot think of the right word, then try using a phrase or a whole sentence to express your idea instead.

Ask Around

If you cannot think of the word that is on the tip of your tongue, then ask around. To anyone who will listen, just say, "Hey, what's the word for ____?" Writers are always glad to help each other.

Freewrite for Three Minutes

You may not be able to think of the right word because you are not certain about what you want to say. To clarify your thinking, try three minutes of freewriting, focusing on the idea you want the word to convey. (Freewriting is explained on page 20.) After the freewriting, try again to come up with the word. You may be able to do so with a better understanding of what you want to express.

Skip the Problem and Return to It Later

When you are drafting, never let any one trouble spot stop your progress. If after a minute you cannot think of the right word, then leave a blank space and push on. You can return to consider the problem again when you revise. When you return, the word may surface, and the problem will be solved. If not, you can try the other strategies in this chapter.

USE SIMPLE, SPECIFIC WORDS

Some people have trouble finding the right words because they think good writing has words like *bumptious, egregious, panacea, parsimonious,* and *pusillanimous* in it. The truth is that good writing is clear, simple, and specific. You do not need the high-flown, 50-dollar words. Instead of *parsimonious,* use *stingy.*

USE THE THESAURUS AND DICTIONARY WISELY

The thesaurus and dictionary are excellent tools for writers seeking the right word. In fact, you may want to invest in a hardback and paperback version of each of these resources. Keep the hardbacks on your writing desk, and carry the paperbacks around with you. One word of caution is in order, however. Be sure you understand the connotation (secondary meaning) of any word you draw from these sources. For example, *skinny* and *lean* may mean the same thing on one level, but because of their connotations, a person would rather be called *lean* than *skinny.* If you do not understand the connotations of a word, you run a risk of misusing it or offending your reader.

USE A COMPUTER

Some word processing programs come with a built-in thesaurus. If yours does not, you can purchase an add-on thesaurus program. Such a program can be handy, but you must be sure you understand the meaning of any word you take from this source.

III

Revising

Because writers usually produce drafts that require a substantial amount of reworking, you will need to study your draft carefully and objectively to discover ways to improve the content, organization, and expression of ideas. This reworking is revising, and it is hard work; however, the procedures described in this section can help you.

9

"My Draft Has Problems."

You've just placed the final period at the end of the last sentence of your first draft, and you're feeling proud of yourself. So you lean back, put your feet up on the desk, and start to reread the masterpiece. However, as you read, your masterpiece doesn't seem nearly as good as you thought it was. Does this mean you have to start over? Probably not. Instead, try some of the suggestions in this chapter.

Be Realistic

Remember, a first draft is called a *rough* draft because your first attempt is supposed to have problems—even lots of them. You should not expect too much too soon. Instead, realize that your first pass is bound to be rough, roll up your sleeves, and get in there and revise until you are happy with the results.

Walk Away

Before deciding about the quality of your draft, leave it for a while to clear your head and regain your objectivity. The longer you stay away, the better; but walk away for at least several hours—for a day if you have the time. When you return to your draft and reread it, you may discover potential that you overlooked previously.

SHARE THE DRAFT

Sometimes writers are too hard on themselves in the early drafting stage. Instead of recognizing the potential in their drafts, they see only the rough spots. As a result, they become frustrated and start over when it is not really necessary. Before deciding about the quality of your draft, share it with several people whose judgment you trust. Ask these readers to note what they like and what they want to hear more about. When you review your readers' comments, you may see how much potential your draft has.

LISTEN TO YOUR DRAFT

Your draft may seem worse than it is if it is messy or written in sloppy handwriting or written in pencil or written on paper ripped out of a spiral notebook. In short, the appearance of the draft may affect your evaluation of it. To judge the worth of your draft more reliably, ask someone to read it to you. As you listen, you may discover sections that are stronger than you realized.

IDENTIFY TWO CHANGES THAT WILL IMPROVE THE DRAFT

If you study your draft and identify two changes that will make it better, you may recognize how much potential your draft has. If you think it will help you judge your draft better, make those changes and *then* decide how you feel about the draft.

WRITE A SECOND DRAFT WITHOUT LOOKING AT THE FIRST

Writing a second draft without looking at the first is often successful because you manage to retain the best parts of the first draft, eliminate the weakest parts, and add some new, effective material. The key is to avoid checking the first draft while writing the second.

DO NOT DESPAIR IF YOU MUST START OVER

Writers start over all the time because often we must discover what we do *not* want to do before we discover what we *do* want to do; *some*times we must learn what we *cannot* do before we are clear about what we *can* do. If you must begin again, do not be discouraged. Your earlier draft or drafts were not a waste of your time—they were groundwork, preliminary efforts that paved the way for your most recent effort.

TRY TO SALVAGE SOMETHING

If you are sure that your draft is awful and you must begin again, at least try to salvage something. Perhaps you can use the same approach to your introduction, or some of your examples, or one main idea. While it is tempting to rip the draft to shreds and begin anew, you may not have to begin at square one. Some of your work may be usable in your new draft.

DO THE BEST YOU CAN WITH WHAT YOU HAVE

Yes, writers start over all the time, but writers do not usually have an unlimited amount of time to work within. At some point you must force yourself to push forward, even if you are not completely comfortable with the status of your first draft. When time is running out, do the best you can with what you have and be satisfied that you have met your deadline.

10

"I Don't Know What to Change."

Good news! You finished your first draft, and you are ready to dig in and make all those changes that will improve your writing and make it fit for a reader. So you read your draft—but wait a minute—everything seems fine. *You* understand what you mean; everything seems clear and well developed to *you*. In fact, you can't figure out what changes to make and what all the fuss about revision is. The suggestions in this chapter can help.

Walk Away

Before revising, the smartest thing you can do is leave your work for a day, or even longer if you can manage it. Getting away from your writing gives you a chance to clear your head and regain your objectivity so that when you return to revise you stand a better chance of identifying necessary changes.

Construct a Reader Profile

As the writer, you may have no trouble figuring out what you meant when you wrote all those words, but that does not guarantee that your reader will have an easy time of it. To revise successfully, you must view your draft as the reader and make changes to meet your reader's needs. Different readers will place different demands on a writer. For example, assume you are writing to convince your reader to vote for a school levy that will increase property taxes. If your audience is someone with children in the school system, explaining that the additional revenue will go toward enhancing the art and music curriculum may be sufficiently persuasive. However, if your reader is a childless retired person on a fixed income, this argument may not be very convincing. Instead, you may need to explain that better schools will cause the reader's home to increase in value so the resale price is higher.

To evaluate your detail from your reader's point of view, construct a reader profile by answering the following 10 questions:

1. How much education does my reader have?

2. What are my reader's age, sex, race, nationality, and religion?

3. What are my reader's occupation and socioeconomic level?

4. What part of the country does my reader live in? Does my reader live in an urban or rural area?

5. What is my reader's political affiliation?

6. How familiar is my reader with my topic?

7. What does my reader need to know to appreciate my point of view?

8. How resistant will my reader be to my point of view?

9. How hard will I have to work to create interest in my topic?

10. Does my reader have any special hobbies or interests or concerns that will affect how my essay is viewed? Is my reader chiefly concerned with money? career? the environment? society? religion? family?

After answering these questions, review your draft with an eye toward providing detail suited to your reader's unique makeup.

THINK LIKE YOUR READER

Asking the following questions as you study your draft can help you think like your reader and identify necessary changes:

1. Is there any place where my reader might lose interest?

2. Is there any place where my reader might not understand what I mean?

3. Is there any place where my reader is not likely to be convinced of the truth of my topic sentence or thesis?

DESCRIBE YOUR DRAFT PARAGRAPH BY PARAGRAPH TO ASSESS WHAT YOU HAVE

Describing your draft paragraph by paragraph can help you analyze its strengths and weaknesses. To do this, summarize the contents of paragraph 1; then explain how that paragraph meets your audience's needs and how it helps you achieve your purpose for writing. Next, summarize the contents of paragraph 2; then explain how that paragraph meets your audience's needs and your purpose. Continue in this fashion until you have described each paragraph. Reading over your description can help you identify points that stray from your thesis, ideas that need more development, and paragraphs that fail to meet a reader's needs or your purpose.

TYPE OR WORD-PROCESS YOUR DRAFT

If you wrote your draft in pen or pencil, type or word-process it into a neat copy, print it out, and then read it over. Problems you overlook in your own handwriting are more apparent in typed form because the copy resembles printed material rather than your own handiwork. As a result, it can be easier to be objective about the writing. Also, some mistakes may leap out at you. For example, a paragraph that ran the better part of a page in your handwritten copy may be only three lines in typed form—a visual signal that more detail may be needed.

LISTEN TO YOUR DRAFT

Often, we can hear problems that we overlook visually. For this reason, you should read your draft out loud at least once. Be sure to go slowly and be careful to read exactly what is on the page. If you read quickly, you are likely to read what you *meant* to write rather than what you actually *did* write.

Some writers do well if they read their drafts into a tape recorder. Then they play back the tape to listen for problems. Still other writers prefer to have other people read their drafts to them. Sometimes, another person's voice helps the writer pick up on problems.

UNDERLINE MAIN POINTS

One way to determine if you have supported your points is to go through your draft and underline every main idea. Then check to see what appears after each underlined point. If one underlined point is immediately followed by another underlined point, you have not supported a main idea. Similarly, if an underlined idea is followed by only one or two sentences, you should consider whether you have enough support. For strategies for supporting points, see Chapter 6.

OUTLINE YOUR DRAFT AFTER WRITING IT

A good way to determine if your ideas follow logically one to the next is to outline your draft *after* writing it. If you have points that do not fit into the outline at the appropriate spots, you have discovered an organization problem.

REVISE IN STAGES

When you revise, you have a great deal to consider. To avoid overlooking important considerations, revise in stages, following one of these patterns.

Easy to Hard.   First make all the easy changes, take a break, and then make the more difficult changes. Take a break whenever you become tired or when you get stuck. Making the easy changes first helps you build enough momentum to carry you through the harder changes.

Hard to Easy.   First make some of your more difficult changes, take a break, make some more of your difficult changes, take another break, and continue with the harder changes, taking breaks as needed. When you have finished the more difficult changes, take a break and tackle the easier changes. Some writers like the psychological lift that comes from getting the hard changes out of the way.

Paragraph by Paragraph.   Revise your first paragraph until it is as perfect as you can make it, and then go on to the next paragraph. Proceed paragraph by paragraph, taking a break after every paragraph or two.

Content–Organization–Effective Expression.   First make all your content changes: adequate detail, relevant detail, specific detail, clarity, and suitable introduction and conclusion. Then take a break and check the organization: logical order of ideas, effective thesis, and clear topic sentences. Take another break and revise for sentence effectiveness: effective word choice, smooth flow, helpful transitions.

SHARE YOUR INTRODUCTION AND CONCLUSION

To judge the effectiveness of your introduction and conclusion, type up these parts separately, and give them to two or three people to read. Ask them whether they would be interested in reading something that opened and closed with these paragraphs.

SHARE YOUR DRAFT WITH A RELIABLE READER

To help them decide what and how to revise, writers often ask reliable readers to respond to their drafts. If you want to consider the opinions of readers when you make revision decisions, you can ask people to complete a questionnaire like the one in Figure 3. To make reader response as valuable as possible, remember the following points:

1. Be sure that the people who read your work are aware of the qualities of effective writing.

2. Be sure that the people who read your work are comfortable giving constructive criticism; do not ask someone to read your work who is reluctant to tell you when something is wrong.

3. Give your readers legible drafts.

4. If you have specific concerns about your draft, mention them to your readers and ask them to speak to those points.

5. Weigh out your readers' responses carefully—do not assume your readers are always correct. If you are in doubt about the value of a response, ask your instructor or a writing center tutor.

6. Talk to your readers and ask them why they responded as they did.

7. Photocopy your draft so it can be read by more than one reader. Look for agreement in the readers' responses.

PRETEND TO BE SOMEONE ELSE

To be more objective about your work so you can decide what to change, pretend you are someone else. Read your draft as the judge of a contest who will award you $10,000 for a prize-winning essay. Or become the editor of a magazine who is deciding what changes to make in the draft before

Figure 3
READER RESPONSE QUESTIONNAIRE

1. Can you easily tell what the thesis is? If so, what is that thesis?

_____

_____

2. Are you interested in reading about this thesis? Why or why not?

_____

_____

3. What do you like best about this essay?

_____

_____

4. Do any points go unproven or unsupported? If so, which ones?

_____

_____

5. Is there anything you do not understand? If so, what?

_____

_____

6. Does the order of ideas make sense? If not, explain the problem.

_____

_____

7. Does any detail stray from the thesis? If so, what?

_____

_____

8. Does the introduction engage your interest? Why or why not?

_____

_____

9. Is the conclusion satisfying? Why or why not?

_____

_____

10. Do you have any advice for the writer that was not covered by the previous questions?

_____

_____

publishing the piece. Or read as your worst enemy, someone who loves to find fault with your work.

USE A REVISING CHECKLIST

Some writers like to use a checklist when they rework their drafts. If you are such a writer, the following checklist may help. The advantages of the checklist are that it helps you proceed in an orderly way, and it keeps you from overlooking some of the revision concerns. In addition, you can combine this checklist with reader response by asking a reliable reader to apply the checklist to your draft.

The page numbers in parentheses refer you to helpful pages in this book.

Content

1. Does your writing have a clear thesis, either stated or implied, that accurately presents your focus? (page 34)

2. Does every point in your writing clearly relate to that thesis? (page 13)

3. Are all your generalizations, including your thesis, adequately supported? (page 13)

4. Are all your points well suited to your audience, purpose, and role? (pages 7 and 8.)

5. Have you avoided stating the obvious? (page 101)

6. Does your introduction create interest in your topic? (page 52)

7. Does your conclusion provide a satisfying ending? (page 65)

Organization

1. Do your ideas follow logically one to the next? (page 14)

2. Do your paragraphs follow logically one to the next? (page 14)

3. Do the details in each paragraph relate to the topic sentence? (page 13)

4. Have you used transitions to show how ideas relate to each other? (page 87)

5. Have you outlined? (page 39)

Expression

1. When you read your work aloud, does everything sound all right? (page 75)

2. Have you avoided wordiness? (page 96)

3. Have you eliminated clichés (overworked expressions)? (page 100)

4. Have you used specific words? (page 99)

5. Did you use a variety of sentence openers? (page 104)

6. Have you used the active voice? (page 100)

7. Have you used action verbs rather than forms of *be?* (page 100)

8. Have you used parallel structures? (page 107)

TRUST YOUR INSTINCTS

Read your draft over and listen to your instincts. When your instincts tell you that something is wrong, you can be reasonably sure that you have come across a problem. Even if you cannot give the problem a name, and even if you are not yet sure what change needs to be made, when you get that feeling that all is not well, you have identified something that needs to be reworked. Most of the time, a writer's instincts are correct.

DO NOT EDIT PREMATURELY

Sometimes writers have trouble deciding what to change because they get bogged down checking commas, spelling, fragments, and the like. However, concerns such as these are matters of correctness, and matters of correctness are best dealt with later, during editing. During revision, you stand a better chance of recognizing what needs to be changed if you focus on content, organization, and effective expression. Do not be distracted by editing concerns too early in the writing process.

USE A COMPUTER

If you wrote your draft on a computer, the following tips may help you decide what changes to make.

Study a Print Copy of Your Draft.   When you view the text on the screen, you see such small portions at a time that you may have trouble getting a good overview of your writing.

Annotate Your Print Copy.*   Put a small square in the margin of your print copy where you make a change as a reminder to add the change to your computer version. When you actually make the change on the computer, place a checkmark in the square. This way, you will not lose track of what changes you have and have not made on each copy.

Put a Checklist in a Window.   If your computer allows you to split the screen, place a revising checklist in a window to refer to as you reread your work. This way, you will be constantly reminded of what to consider while revising. Either make up your own checklist, or copy the one on page 83.

Highlight Areas with Boldface Type.   If you are unsure about parts of your draft, use boldface to highlight the areas in question. Then print out your draft and give it to two or more reliable readers (see page 81) and ask them to react to the parts in boldface type.

Keep a Scrap Pile.   Rather than permanently delete material you cut or revise, copy and move it to a new file. Who knows? You may decide later that you want to use that material in a different spot or altered form.

*Thanks to John M. Green for this suggestion.

11

"My Ideas Seem All Mixed Up."

Okay, let's say you finish your draft, and you're feeling confident until you read it over—or a reliable reader does—and you discover that your ideas do not seem connected to each other. Everything is a jumble. Does this mean your ideas are no good? Absolutely not. It just means that when you revise, you should consider the suggestions in this chapter.

Use Topic Sentences

A *topic sentence* presents the main idea of a paragraph. All the details in a paragraph must relate clearly and directly to that topic sentence (see page 11). If your ideas seem mixed up, check to be sure you are using topic sentences to focus your body paragraphs. If you are not, add them. Then compare every sentence in each body paragraph against its topic sentence to be sure that everything relates to that topic sentence. If something does not relate directly, it must be deleted or moved to another paragraph where it fits better.

Write a Postdraft Outline

You can outline your draft *after* it is written to check the organization. To do this, fill in an outline map, outline tree, outline worksheet, or formal outline with the ideas already written in the draft. (See Chapter 3.) If you discover points that do not fit logically into a particular section of the outline, you have an organization problem that needs your attention.

USE TRANSITIONS

Transitions are words and phrases that show how ideas relate to each other. Sometimes when your ideas seem mixed up, you just need to supply appropriate transitions to demonstrate the connections between points. Consider, for example, these sentences:

> Today's economy is not good for the stock market. There is still money to be made in speculative stocks.

Without a transitional word or phrase, the reader can have a difficult time seeing how the ideas in the two sentences relate to each other. Add a transition, and this problem is solved:

> Today's economy is not good for the stock market. <u>Nevertheless</u>, there is still money to be made in speculative stocks.

The following transitions can help you demonstrate how your ideas relate to each other:

also	later	however	in like fashion
and	earlier	on the contrary	consequently
in addition	at the same time	on the other hand	as a result
furthermore	for example	yet	therefore
moreover	for instance	although	nevertheless
indeed	in other words	even though	for this reason
in fact	in short	in the same way	in summary
near	similarly	in conclusion	in front of
now	next to	then	thus

REPEAT KEY WORDS

You can often demonstrate how ideas relate to each other by repeating a key word or words, like this:

> The Senate is scheduled to vote on the tax reform <u>bill</u> Wednesday. This <u>bill</u> will reduce taxes.

REPEAT KEY IDEAS

You can also demonstrate how ideas relate to each other by repeating a key idea, like this:

> The Senate is scheduled to vote on the tax reform <u>bill</u> Wednesday. This <u>legislation</u> will reduce taxes.

USE OUTLINE CARDS

Write your thesis and each of your main ideas on a separate index card. To experiment with alternate orders, arrange and rearrange the cards until your ideas progress in the best order.

USE A COMPUTER

If your ideas seem mixed up, the computer can provide assistance.

Copy and Rearrange Your Draft

Make a copy of your draft in a new file. Then use the cut and paste functions to try your paragraphs in a new order.

Boldface Your Thesis and Topic Sentences

Your ideas may seem confused because you have a relevance problem in one or more paragraphs. Check every boldfaced topic sentence against your thesis to be sure each is clearly related. Then check every sentence in your body paragraphs to be sure each is relevant to its boldfaced topic sentence. If you find something that is not relevant, delete it or revise to make it relevant.

The Postdraft Outline

After writing your draft, save the file. Then create a second copy of the draft in a new file. Reduce this second copy to an outline by identifying in each paragraph the sentence that states the major idea (the topic sentence) and the major supporting details; strip everything else from each paragraph (using the delete key or a block erase), leaving just the sentences that give the main ideas and major supporting details.

Next, identify your thesis sentence and write it at the top of your outline. Now use roman and arabic numbers, capital and lowercase letters to sequence the sentences following the thesis sentence into a formal outline. Study this outline and make any necessary adjustments.

Once you have made and adjusted the outline, you can place it in a window and then recall the original draft and revise it according to the insights gained from making the outline. Or you can print the outline and use it as a revision guide.

12

"My Draft Is Too Short."

Sometimes you think you have enough ideas to get under way, so you start drafting. Later, you come to the end and place a period after your last sentence. Then you look back over your work, and you come to the disheartening recognition that your draft is much too short, and you have already said everything you can think of. What do you do? No, you do not throw yourself in front of a high-speed train. Instead, you try one of the strategies in this chapter.

Underline Major Points

Go through your draft and underline every major point. Then check to see how much you have written after each underlined point. If one underlined point is immediately followed by another underlined point, you have neglected to develop an idea. Adding supporting detail after one or more of your major points can solve your length problem. (See Chapter 6 for ways to add supporting detail.)

When you add detail, do not state the obvious or provide unrelated information, or you will be guilty of *padding*—writing useless material just to bulk up the piece. Padding irritates readers by requiring them to read unnecessary material. Let's assume that you are writing to explain how schools foster competition, rather than cooperation, in students. If you say that schools have students compete for grades, compete for positions on sports teams, compete for student government, compete for scholarships, and compete for cheerleading, you would be providing helpful examples that illustrate your point. However, if you give a dictionary definition of *competition* as "the act of struggling to win some prize, honor, or advantage," you would be padding your essay with information your reader already knows.

SHOW AFTER YOU TELL

If your draft is too short, you may be *telling* your reader things are true without *showing* that they are true. Remember to "show; don't just tell." Consider the following:

> I have always hated winter. For one thing, the cold bothers me. For another, daily living becomes too difficult.

The previous sentences are an example of telling without showing. Here is a revision with detail added to *show:*

> I have always hated winter. For one thing, the cold bothers me. Even in the house with the furnace running, I can never seem to get warm. I wear a turtleneck under a heavy wool sweater and drink one cup of hot tea after another in a futile effort to ease the chill that goes to my bones. A simple trip to the mailbox at the street leaves me chattering for an hour. My hands go numb, and my nose and ears sting from the cold. The doctor explained that I cannot tolerate the cold because I have a circulation problem which causes my capillaries to spasm, interrupting the blood flow to my extremities. I also hate winter because daily living becomes too difficult. Snow and ice are tracked into the house, necessitating frequent cleanups. Snow must be shoveled to get the car out of the driveway. Icy walks make walking treacherous, and driving to the grocery store becomes a dangerous endeavor thanks to slick, snow-covered roads.

ADD DESCRIPTION

Description can add interest and liveliness, and it can help your reader form clear mental images. To flesh out an essay, look for opportunities to describe a person or scene. For more on description, see page 59.

ADD EXAMPLES

Examples help clarify matters for a reader and make things more specific. As you work to lengthen a draft, look for general statements that can be illustrated with a well-chosen example or two. For more on examples, see pages 59–60.

Add Conversation

Sometimes you can enliven an essay by adding the words that were spoken. Consider, for example, the following paragraph:

> I stepped up to the plate, ready to swing away, but the catcher kept saying things to shake my confidence. I tried to ignore him and keep my focus, but the next thing I knew, I was too nervous to swing at all. The pitcher threw three pitches; the umpire called three strikes; and I walked to the outfield feeling like a fool.

Notice, now, how much more full-bodied the paragraph is with the addition of some conversation:

> I stepped up to the plate, ready to swing away, but the catcher kept saying things to shake my confidence. "I hope you don't choke like the last time," he sneered as I tapped the bat against the inside of my shoe. "Move in; easy out," he shouted to the outfield as I assumed my batting stance. I tried to ignore him and keep my focus, but the next thing I knew, I was too nervous to swing at all. "I figured you'd choke, you big baby," he sneered after the first called strike. The pitcher threw three pitches; the umpire called three strikes; and I walked to the outfield feeling like a fool.

Evaluate the Significance of a Point

In addition to stating a point, go on to explain the importance, impact, or meaning of that point—in short, its significance. For example, assume you are arguing that the proposed site for the new state prison on the north end of town is not a good choice. You could go on to explain the significance of the choice of site:

> The proposed site on the north end of town is favored by state legislators, not because it is inherently the best site, but because their wealthy campaign contributors want the building as far away from their residences as possible. The legislators fear angering their wealthy supporters because they do not want to lose their financial assistance in future campaigns.

Share Your Draft with a Reliable Reader

Ask someone with good judgment about writing to review your draft and suggest where and what kind of detail is needed. For a detailed discussion of using a reliable reader, see page 81.

RETURN TO IDEA GENERATION

Your draft may be too short because you began writing before you generated enough ideas to write about. If you have a favorite idea generation technique, try it now. If it lets you down, try one or more of the other techniques described in Chapter 1. Writers frequently step back to idea generation before going forward, so interrupting your drafting is not something you should either resist or worry about.

CHECK YOUR THESIS

Study your thesis to see if it too severely limits the territory you can cover. If so, broaden the thesis a bit so that you can cover more ground and thereby increase the length of your draft. Let's say, for example, that your draft has this thesis:

> High school athletics teaches adolescents to be self-reliant.

If you have exhausted everything you can say about how high school athletics teaches self-reliance, if you have tried all the techniques in this chapter, and if you still only have a page and a half of material, consider expanding your thesis to allow discussion of other points:

> High school athletics teaches adolescents to be self-reliant. Interestingly, however, athletics also teaches young people how to be team players.

Now you can expand the draft by discussing two advantages of high school athletics rather than one.

A word of caution is in order here: Do not get carried away when you expand your thesis, or you will be forced into covering too much territory. Consider how difficult it would be to provide an adequately detailed discussion of this expanded thesis:

> High school athletics teaches adolescents everything they need to know to succeed as adults: how to be self-reliant, how to be a team player, how to function under pressure, how to accept criticism, and how to give 100 percent.

An essay with this thesis is destined to fail in one of two ways. Either it will be so long that the reader will feel overwhelmed, or it will provide only superficial treatment of the main points.

Use a Computer

Before each of your main points, press the insert key and then hit the space bar 10 times. This should visually separate each main point and its support. Once each main point and its support are separated from the rest of the essay, you can study each point and support individually to determine if you can add an example, a story, a conversation, or a description. After adding detail to develop the main points, rejoin your sentences to form a longer draft.

13

"My Draft Is Too Long."

Perhaps you find yourself writing page after page after page—all the while feeling great because you have so much to say. Unfortunately, longer is not necessarily better. Your reader's time is valuable, so keep your writing to a length that will not unduly tax your audience. If you find that your draft is too long, try the strategies given here.

Check Your Thesis

Look for ways to narrow the scope of your thesis. If your thesis takes in too much territory, you will be forced to cover too many points, and the result will be a very long piece of writing. Here is a thesis that calls for a very long piece:

> The amount of violence on television, in the movies, and in popular fiction is alarming.

To discuss television, movie, and book violence in adequate detail would require many, many pages. A more manageable piece of writing would result from a thesis like this:

> The amount of violence in prime-time network television is alarming.

ELIMINATE UNNECESSARY POINTS

If your draft is too long, check to be sure you are not making unnecessary points. For example, assume you are writing a report on the mutual funds that provide the best retirement income. If you are writing for your boss, who is an investment banker, it would be silly to define the term *mutual funds.* However, if you are writing a newspaper article for readers who may not know what mutual funds are, a definition would be helpful. Similarly, if you are comparing two kinds of bicycles, you should not mention that both have two tires, as this would be stating the obvious.

OUTLINE YOUR DRAFT

Even if you outlined before drafting, outline your draft after you write it. Then check the outline to be sure you are not repeating points or including irrelevant detail. Be sure all your details are relevant to both the topic and the opinion expressed in your thesis. (See page 13.)

ELIMINATE WORDINESS

Often you can cut your draft down to size by eliminating wordiness in the following ways:

1. Eliminate repetition.

Wordy: My biggest problem and concern was how to pay next month's rent. (Problem and concern are repetitious.)

Better: My biggest problem was how to pay next month's rent.

Better: My biggest concern was how to pay next month's rent.

2. Eliminate deadwood (words that add no meaning).

Deadwood	Better
the color green	green
mix together	mix
past history	past
end result	result
important essentials	essentials

Wordy: I cannot concentrate unless I am alone by myself.

Better: I cannot concentrate unless I am alone.

Better: I cannot concentrate unless I am by myself.

3. **Pare down wordy phrases.**

Wordy	Better
in this day and age	now
in society today	today
being that	since
due to the fact that	because
for the purpose of	so

Wordy: At this point in time, I do not think we can afford the rate increase.

Better: I do not think we can afford the rate increase now.

4. **Reduce the number of phrases.**

Wordy: The shortage of skilled labor in this country points to the need for a greater number of vocational education programs.

Better: This country's skilled labor shortage points to a needed increase in vocational education programs.

5. **Reduce the number of "that" clauses.**

Wordy: The reporters asked the senator to repeat the explanation that she gave earlier.

Better: The reporters asked the senator to repeat her earlier explanation.

DO NOT OVERWRITE YOUR INTRODUCTION OR CONCLUSION

Check your introduction and conclusion to be sure one or both are not overly long. Remember, these parts of an essay are meant only to pave the way for your main discussion and tie things off at the end.

USE A COMPUTER

The following suggestions can help you find ways to shorten a draft that is too long.

Separate Your Sentences

Hit the enter key after each sentence to reformat your writing into a list of sentences. With your sentences listed, you may find it easier to check them for wordiness.

Use the Word Count Feature

Highlight each paragraph separately and use the word count feature to determine the number of words in each paragraph. If one paragraph is significantly longer than the others, check it for irrelevant detail.

CHAPTER

14

"MY WRITING SEEMS BORING."

"I couldn't put it down!" "A real page-turner!" "A must read!" No, these are not the exclamations people must make about your writing, but you do have a responsibility to hold your reader's interest. If your draft seems boring, try the strategies described in this chapter to improve your detail and style.

REPLACE GENERAL WORDS WITH SPECIFIC ONES

To add interest, replace general words with more specific ones. Here are two sentences. The first has general words, which are underlined; the second has specific words, which are also underlined. Which sentence is more interesting?

General words: The <u>car went</u> down the <u>street</u>.

Specific words: The <u>red Corvette streaked</u> down <u>Dover Avenue</u>.

You probably found the second sentence more interesting because of its more specific word choice.

The following chart will give you a clearer idea of the difference between general and specific words.

General	Specific	General	Specific
car	1989 Buick	dog	mangy collie
sweater	yellow cardigan	hat	Phillies cap
			Continued

General	Specific	General	Specific
shoes	Nike hightops	speak	mumble
feel good	feel optimistic	book	*Angela's Ashes*
walk	saunter	drink	slurp
cry	sob loudly	said	snapped
house	two-story colonial	rain	pounding rain
a lot	twelve	later	in two days

USE ACTIVE VOICE

To give your writing more energy, rewrite sentences so that their subjects perform the actions indicated by the verbs. Then your sentences will be in the *active voice.* Here is an example:

> The labor leader negotiated a new contract for the autoworkers. (The action suggested by the verb *negotiated* is performed by the subject, *labor leader.*)

When the subject does not perform the verb's action (putting the sentence in the *passive voice*), the sentence has less energy:

> The new contract for the autoworkers was negotiated by the labor leader. (The subject *the new contract* does not perform the action of the verb *negotiated.*)

SUBSTITUTE ACTION VERBS FOR FORMS OF *TO BE*

Forms of *to be (am, is, are, was, were)* have less energy and interest than action verbs, so when possible use action verbs, like this:

Less energy: Mayor Daley <u>was</u> always a believer in party politics.
More energy: Mayor Daley always <u>believed</u> in party politics.

REWRITE CLICHÉS

Clichés are tired, overworked expressions. At one time the expressions were fresh and interesting, but because of overuse, they have become boring. Here is a representative sampling of clichés:

cold as ice	free as a bird	sadder but wiser
high as a kite	last but not least	green with envy
fresh as a daisy	stiff as a board	hard as nails
under the weather	bull in a china shop	raining cats and dogs
in the same boat	the last straw	smart as a whip

To add interest, replace clichés with original phrasings. Here is an example:

Cliché: When the police officer pulled me over for speeding, I was shaking like a leaf.

Revision: When the police officer pulled me over for speeding, I was trembling with anxiety.

ELIMINATE STATEMENTS OF THE OBVIOUS

Stating the obvious makes writing boring. Let's say that you are arguing that young people should not be permitted to watch more than an hour of television a day. A sentence like the following will bore a reader because some of what it says is so obvious it does not need to be said at all.

Television, an electronic device for bringing sound and pictures into the home, can be a positive or negative influence on our children, depending on how it is used.

To make your writing more interesting, eliminate statements of the obvious:

Television may influence our children for good or ill, depending on how it is used.

INCLUDE CONVERSATION

Including the words people spoke is a good way to enliven writing, especially when you are telling a story, because conversation adds interest and immediacy. For more on conversation, see page 92.

ADD DESCRIPTION

Description adds vitality and interest, so look for opportunities to describe something: a scene, a person's clothing, a facial expression, a tone of voice, the brightness of the sun, the feel of a handshake. The description need not be elaborate, nor should it distract the reader from your main point. For example, if you are telling the story of a first encounter, some description can add liveliness, like this:

> The door was open and I saw Dr. Harkness hunched over his desk, his nose on the paper he was studying, his eyes squinted into slits. I knocked on the door frame to get his attention, but the barely perceptible sound was too much for him. He jerked upright, startled by the intrusion. When he saw me, he brushed wisps of white hair from his eyes, smoothed his red and blue flannel shirt, and smiled sheepishly. "How can I help you, young man?" he asked, as he lifted his bulky frame from the chair.

ADD EXAMPLES

Examples add interest because they take the general and make it specific. Look for opportunities to follow a general point with a specific example. For instance, if you say that Lee is a scatterbrain, go on to show this by giving the example of the time Lee locked the keys in the car three times in one day.

TELL A STORY

A brief story can add interest and help establish a point by serving as an example. For instance, assume you are explaining that being a student *and* a parent can get very complicated. Also assume that one point you make is that sometimes the two roles conflict with each other. To establish this point, you could tell the story of the time your six-year-old woke up sick three hours before your history exam and you had to get her to the doctor, arrange for a baby-sitter, pick up a prescription—and still make it to class on time.

CHECK YOUR THESIS

If your thesis takes in too much territory, you can be forced into a superficial, general discussion—and such discussions are boring. For example, consider this thesis:

Professional sports should be reformed.

An essay that adequately covers all professional sports and all areas that could benefit from reform is likely to involve a superficial discussion because anything in-depth will lead to a very long piece. If your thesis is too ambitious, pare it down, like this:

> During the off-season as well as the playing season, athletes should have to submit to random drug testing.

Now you can provide a much more interesting discussion because you can give specifics and still have a piece that is a manageable length.

USE A COMPUTER

Use your word processing program's search-and-replace function to find general words you are in the habit of using. For example, you can ask the computer to spot where you have used these general words: *very, quite, a lot, rather, really, great, good, bad,* and *some.* Once the computer has located these words, you can decide whether to retain one or more of them or rewrite to be more specific.

15

"How Can I Get My Writing to Flow?"

Read this paragraph out loud. It sounds choppy. It does not flow. The style seems immature. It sounds like it was written by someone's kid brother. This is my way of showing that lack of flow is bad. Is it working?

Actually, you do not always have to read your work aloud to detect a lack of flow. When you read silently, the words "sound" in your brain, allowing you to "hear" this problem. Then you can eliminate it with the techniques described in this chapter.

Use Different Sentence Openers

Writing sounds choppy or singsong when too many sentences in a row begin the same way. For example, the first paragraph of this chapter sounds choppy because most of the sentences begin with the subject. The solution is to mix the following sentence openings.

1. **Open with a descriptive word (a *modifier*).**

   <u>Strangely</u>, little Billy did not enjoy his birthday.

   <u>Confused</u>, the stranger asked directions to a bus stop.

   <u>Melting</u>, the ice formed slushy puddles on the pavement.

2. **Open with a descriptive phrase (a *modifier*).**

   <u>Despite my better judgment</u>, I bought a ticket for the roller coaster ride.

   <u>Hiding in the living room</u>, twelve of us waited for the right moment to leap out and yell, "Surprise!"

   <u>Pleased by her grade on the physics exam</u>, Loretta treated herself to a special dinner.

   <u>Under the couch</u>, the wet dog hid from her owner.

3. **Open with a *subordinate clause* (a dependent word group with a subject and verb).**

   <u>When Congress announced its budget reform package</u>, members of both political parties offered their support.

   <u>If the basketball team can recruit a power forward</u>, we will have all the ingredients for a winning season.

   <u>Before you contribute to a charity</u>, check the identification of the person requesting the money.

4. **Open with *to* and the verb (an *infinitive*).**

   <u>To protect</u> our resources, we must all recycle.

   <u>To convince</u> my parents to buy me a car, I had to agree to pay the car insurance.

   <u>To gain</u> five pounds by the start of wrestling season, Luis doubled his intake of carbohydrates.

5. **Open with the subject.**

   <u>Losses</u> led gains in today's stock market activity.

   <u>Corvina's goal</u> is to become the youngest manager in the company's history.

   <u>The curtains</u> were dulled by years of accumulated dirt.

VARY THE PLACEMENT OF TRANSITIONS

Transitions are words and phrases that link ideas and show how they relate to each other. (Transitions are discussed on page 87.) One way to improve flow is to vary the placement of transitions.

Transition at the beginning:	<u>In addition</u>, providing child care in the workplace is a good idea because half of all mothers now work.
Transition in the middle:	Jan's opinion, <u>on the other hand</u>, is that child-care programs will cost too much.
Transition at the end:	Many employers now offer day care as a benefit, <u>however</u>.

COMBINE SHORT SENTENCES

When you hear choppiness, look to see if you have two or more short sentences in a row. If so, combine at least two of those short sentences into a longer one, using one of these words:

and	or	for	yet
but	nor	so	because

Short sentences (choppy):	The house was well constructed. It was decorated badly.
Combined sentence (smoother):	The house was well constructed, but it was decorated badly.
Short sentences (choppy):	The police and fire fighters both needed money. They combined their resources in a fund-raiser.
Combined sentence (smoother):	The police and fire fighters both needed money, so they combined their resources in a fund-raiser.

FOLLOW LONG SENTENCES WITH SHORT ONES AND SHORT SENTENCES WITH LONG ONES

The following examples alternate long and short sentences. As you read them, notice how well they flow.

Short followed
by long: The coach jumped to his feet. Although he had been coaching for 20 years, he had never before seen such a perfectly executed play.

Long followed
by short: This city needs a mayor who knows how to deal effectively with city council and how to trim waste from the municipal budget. This city needs Dale Davidson.

USE PARALLEL CONSTRUCTIONS

To maintain flow, keep series items *parallel* by putting them in the same grammatical form.

Not parallel: Coach Rico values teamwork, sportsmanship, and she values effort.

Parallel: Coach Rico values teamwork, sportsmanship, and effort.

Not parallel: The offensive television commercial insults women, glamorizes drinking, and it diminishes the importance of the family.

Parallel: The offensive television commercial insults women, glamorizes drinking, and diminishes the importance of the family.

USE YOUR EAR

Read your writing aloud with a pen in your hand. Where you hear that it is not flowing well, place a check mark. Then go back and try the techniques described in this chapter to ease the flow where you have placed the check marks.

IV

EDITING

Errors in grammar, spelling, punctuation, and capitalization present a special problem because mistakes are distracting, and they can cause your reader to lose confidence in your ability. For this reason, you have a responsibility to find and correct your errors. This process is editing. For most writers, it makes sense to edit last, after all the other changes have been made. This way you are not checking something that you may ultimately strike from the paper anyway. When you do edit, the procedures described in the next chapters can help.

16

"I Need Help Finding My Mistakes."

You may be wondering what the big deal is about grammar, usage, and spelling mistakes. You may be thinking that as long as your reader can understand what you mean, it doesn't matter if you misspell words, get punctuation wrong, or choose incorrect verbs. Well, if you're writing to your best friend or your mother, the truth is that it probably doesn't make much difference because those people will have a high opinion of you, no matter what. However, for almost all other readers, mistakes do make a difference. They can distract a reader's attention away from your content, and they can cause your reader to doubt your ability.

Edit Last

The time to *edit* (find and correct mistakes) is near the end of your writing process. During idea generation, drafting, and revising, mistakes have not been an issue because you have been focusing on content. If you edit during these stages, you may look up the spelling of a word that you eliminate during revision or check a comma in a sentence that never makes it to the final draft. However, once done with revising, you can scrutinize your draft for errors.

Leave Your Work for a While

By the time you are ready to look for errors, you may not have a fresh enough perspective to notice mistakes. To compensate for this, you should leave your writing for a day to clear your head. When you return to your work, you should have a sharper eye for spotting errors.

POINT TO EACH WORD AND PUNCTUATION MARK

Go over your writing *very* slowly. If you build up even a little speed, you can overlook errors because you will see what you *intended* to write rather than what you actually *did* write. This is because you know so well what you want to say that you see it on the page whether it is there or not. One way to ensure that you move slowly is to point to each word and punctuation mark and study each one a second or two. Be sure to read what you are pointing to; it is tempting to move your finger or pen ahead of what you are reading, which causes you to build up speed and miss mistakes.

USE A RULER

Place a ruler under the first line of your writing and examine that line for mistakes one word at a time. Then drop the ruler down a line and examine that line for mistakes. This way, you may have better luck finding errors for two reasons. First, you are less likely to build up speed and miss mistakes. Second, the ruler prevents the words below the line from entering your visual field and distracting you.

PREPARE A FRESH, TYPED OR WORD-PROCESSED COPY OF YOUR DRAFT

Because handwriting can be hard on the eyes, errors can be spotted more easily in type. Also, you can be more objective about typed or word-processed copy because it seems more like printed materials—more like someone else's writing.

LISTEN TO YOUR DRAFT

Sometimes you can hear mistakes that you overlook visually. Have someone read your draft to you, read it aloud to yourself, or speak it into a tape recorder and play back the tape. If you read your draft to yourself or into a tape recorder, be sure to read *exactly* what is on the page. Remember, writers tend to read what they *meant* to say rather than what they *did* say. Also, remember that some mistakes, such as certain misspellings, cannot be heard, so listening should be combined with visual editing.

Learn Your Pattern of Error

We all make mistakes, but we do not all make the *same* mistakes. One person may misspell words often, another may write run-on sentences, another may have trouble choosing the correct verb, and so on. Be aware of the kinds of mistakes you make so you can make a special effort to locate those errors. In fact, edit one extra time for each of the mistakes you have a tendency to make.

Once you know the kinds of mistakes you make, you may be able to determine under what circumstances you make those mistakes. For example, once you discover that you have trouble choosing verbs, a little study of your writing may tell you that you have this trouble whenever you begin a sentence with *there is* or *there are.* This is valuable information because it tells you to check the verbs in any sentences that begin with these words.

Use an Editing Checklist

An editing checklist can ensure that you are attending to everything. Use the one below or devise your own checklist of errors you are in the habit of making.

✔ NOTE: *The page numbers in parentheses refer you to helpful pages in the book.*

1. Have you read your work aloud to listen for problems? (page 111)

2. Did you check every possible misspelling in a dictionary or with a spell checker? (page 148)

3. Did you edit for run-on sentences and comma splices? (page 121)

4. Did you edit for sentence fragments? (page 115)

5. Did you check your use of verbs? (page 131)

6. Did you check your use of pronouns? (page 124)

7. Did you check your use of modifiers? (page 135)

8. Have you checked any punctuation you are unsure of? (pages 139 and 144)

9. Have you checked your use of capital letters?

Trust Your Instincts

Maybe you have had this experience: You have a feeling that something is wrong. However, you cannot give the problem a name, and you are not sure how to solve it, so you just skip over it and hope your reader does not notice. Then you submit your writing, and sure enough—your reader was troubled by the same thing you were troubled by. If you have had this experience, you learned that your instincts are reliable. When that nagging feeling tells you a problem exists, trust the feeling and assume that something is wrong. Because much of what you know about language has been internalized, an inner alarm may sound when you have made a mistake. Always heed that alarm, even if you are not sure what the problem is or how to solve it. Get help if necessary for diagnosing and eliminating the error.

EDIT MORE THAN ONCE

Because it is so easy to overlook errors, edit more than once. Many writers edit once for anything they can find and a separate time for each of the kinds of errors they have a tendency to make.

WHEN IN DOUBT, CHECK IT OUT

Invest in a grammar handbook, and when you are unsure about something, look it up. You can buy a grammar handbook, either large or small, in your college bookstore.

LEARN THE RULES

You cannot edit confidently if you do not know the rules. Many people think the grammar and usage rules are understood only by English teachers, but the truth is that anyone can learn them. Invest in a grammar handbook, and each time you make an error, learn the appropriate rule so that mistake does not happen again.

GET SOME HELP

Professional writers have editors who locate and correct errors that get by them, and you can get some help too. Ask someone to go over your writing to find mistakes that you overlooked. Be sure, however, that the person who helps you edit is someone who knows grammar and usage rules; otherwise, you will not get reliable information. If your school has a writing center, you may be able to stop in there for reliable editing assistance. Please keep in mind, though, that the ultimate responsibility for editing is yours. You must learn and apply the rules on your own, with only backup help from others.

USE A COMPUTER

The following techniques may help you edit with your computer.

Put Your Editing Checklist into a Window. Split your screen, and place your editing checklist (either the one on page 112 or one you devise) into a window. Consult the checklist as you edit.

Quadruple-Space Your Text. Reformat your text with four spaces between each line. This way, you can edit one line at a time with less text entering your visual field to distract you from the words you are studying.

Edit the Screen and the Paper Copy. Edit twice. The first time through, edit by studying the words on the screen, making the necessary changes as you go. Then print your text and edit a second time on the paper copy. Enter these changes into your file and print a fresh copy.

Use the Computer's Search Function to Locate Trouble Spots. For example, if you habitually misuse semicolons and confuse *to* and *too,* find every semicolon, *to,* and *too* in your draft and check your usage.

Use Your Computer's Grammar Check with Caution. They are not always correct. Therefore, you must evaluate their advice and carefully edit on your own.

17

"I USED A PERIOD AND A CAPITAL LETTER, SO WHY ISN'T THIS A SENTENCE?"

You can put a saddle on a donkey, but that won't make it a horse. Similarly, you can start a word group with a capital letter and end it with a period, question mark, or exclamation point, but that won't necessarily make it a sentence. No matter how you dress it up, a word group will not be a sentence unless it has three things: a subject, a complete verb, and a sense of completeness. If any one of those three things is missing, you cannot have a sentence. Even if you add a capital letter and end punctuation to a word group missing one of these, you *still* don't have a sentence; instead, you have a *sentence fragment.*

Sometimes sentence fragments are used to achieve a special effect, but most often you should avoid them because they can confuse a reader.

Sentence fragment:	The child rolled over. Then fell asleep.
Explanation:	Despite the period and capital letter, *then fell asleep* is not a sentence. It is a sentence fragment because the subject is missing.
Correction:	The child rolled over. Then he fell asleep. (A subject is added.)
Sentence fragment:	Although the election was close. The losing candidate did not ask for a recount.
Explanation:	Despite the period and capital letter, *although the election was close* is not a sentence. It is a sentence fragment because it lacks a sense of completeness.

Correction:	Although the election was close, the losing candidate did not ask for a recount. (The fragment is joined to the sentence.)
Sentence fragment:	Maria has many admirable traits. Such as loyalty, creativity, and integrity.
Explanation:	Despite the period and capital letter, *such as loyalty, creativity, and integrity* is not a sentence. It is a fragment because it lacks both a subject and verb.
Correction:	Maria has many admirable traits, such as loyalty, creativity, and integrity. (The fragment is joined to the sentence.)

If you have trouble editing for sentence fragments, the tips in the rest of this chapter should help you.

ISOLATE EVERYTHING YOU ARE CALLING A SENTENCE

Start at the beginning of your draft and place one finger of your left hand under the capital letter. Then place a finger of your right hand under the period, question mark, or exclamation point. Now read the word group between your fingers. Does it sound as if something is missing? If so, you probably have a sentence fragment.

Move through your entire draft this way, isolating word groups with your fingers and reading them. Each time you hear a fragment, stop and make the necessary correction. This procedure is time-consuming, but the payoff is worth the investment of time.

✔ *HINT: Some people have more success if they read the word groups out loud.*

READ YOUR DRAFT BACKWARD

Read your last sentence; pause for a moment to hear if something is missing, and then read the next-to-the-last sentence, again pausing to listen for something missing. Proceed this way until you have worked back to the first sentence. Each time you hear that something is missing, stop and correct the fragment you have found.

CHECK *-ING* AND *-ED* VERB FORMS

Sometimes sentence fragments result when *-ing* or *-ed* verb forms stand by themselves. Here are two examples with the *-ing* and *-ed* verb forms underlined.

Fragment: The kitten <u>stretching</u> after her nap.

Fragment: The child <u>frustrated</u> by the complicated toy.

To correct fragments that result when *-ing* or *-ed* verbs stand alone, pick an appropriate verb from this list and add it to the *-ing* or *-ed* form:

is	was	have	had
are	were	has	

Fragment: The kittens <u>stretching</u> after their naps.

Sentence: The kittens <u>are stretching</u> after their naps.

Sentence: The kittens <u>were stretching</u> after their naps.

Fragment: The child <u>frustrated</u> by the complicated toy.

Sentence: The child <u>is frustrated</u> by the complicated toy.

Sentence: The child <u>was frustrated</u> by the complicated toy.

To find fragments that result when *-ing* or *-ed* verbs stand alone, go through your draft checking each *-ing* and *-ed* verb form. Read the sentence with the form and ask if a verb from the above list is necessary for a sense of completeness. Sometimes, as in the following example, an *-ed* verb can stand alone:

Sentence: The kittens <u>stretched</u> after their naps.

CHECK FOR FRAGMENT WARNING WORDS

The following words often begin sentence fragments:

after	before	such as
although	especially	unless
as	even though	until
as if	for example	when
as long as	if	whenever
as soon as	in order to	where
as though	since	wherever
because	so that	while

Read aloud every word group that begins with one of the above words or phrases and listen carefully to hear if something is missing. Do not assume that anything beginning with one of these fragment warning words is automatically a sentence fragment because sentences, too, can begin with these words and phrases. To be sure, read aloud to hear if something is missing.

Sentence: While Rudy cleaned the house, Sue cooked dinner. (When you read these words out loud, there is no sense that something is missing.)

Fragment: While Rudy cleaned the house. (When you read these words out loud, you can hear that something is missing.)

WATCH OUT FOR *WHO, WHOM, WHOSE, WHICH,* AND *WHERE*

If you begin a word group with *who, whom, whose, which,* or *where* without asking a question, you most likely have written a sentence fragment.

Sentence: Who lives next door?

Fragment: Who lives next door.

Sentence: Whose advice have I valued over the years?

Fragment: Whose advice I have valued over the years.

Look at any word group that begins with *who, whom, whose, which,* or *where* and be sure that word group is asking a question. If it is not, join the word group to the sentence before it, as illustrated here:

Sentence
and fragment: Stavros is a good friend. <u>Whose advice I have valued over the years</u>.

Sentence: Stavros is a good friend, whose advice I have valued over the years.

ELIMINATE THE FRAGMENTS

The above techniques will help you locate sentence fragments; the next two techniques will help you eliminate fragments once you find them. Keep in mind that no one technique will work for every fragment, so if one correction method does not work, try the other.

Join the Fragment to a Sentence before or after It

Sentence and fragment:	The custom of hat-tipping goes back to the knights. <u>Who</u> would remove their helmets before a lord.
Fragment joined to sentence:	The custom of hat-tipping goes back to the knights, who would remove their helmets before a lord.
Fragment and sentence:	<u>While trying on the cashmere sweater.</u> Molly snagged the sleeve with her class ring.
Fragment joined to sentence:	While trying on the cashmere sweater, Molly snagged the sleeve with her class ring.

Add the Missing Word or Words

To eliminate a fragment that results when a subject or all or part of the verb is left out, add the missing word or words.

Sentence and fragment:	The auto mechanic assured us the repairs would be minor. <u>Then proceeded to list a dozen things wrong with the car.</u>
Fragment eliminated with addition of the missing subject *he:*	The auto mechanic assured us the repairs would be minor. Then he proceeded to list a dozen things wrong with the car.
Fragment:	The Surgeon General announcing new nutritional guidelines.
Fragment eliminated with addition of the missing part of the verb *is:*	The Surgeon General is announcing new nutritional guidelines.
Sentence and fragment:	Police chiefs want to hire more officers. <u>However, not without additional funds.</u>

Fragment eliminated
with addition of
the missing subject
and verb: Police chiefs want to hire more officers. However,
they cannot do so without additional funds.

Use a Computer

Press the enter key before each capital letter that marks the start of a sentence to reformat your paper into a list of sentences. Then read each word group separately to hear if something is missing. Because each word group is now physically separated, finding fragments can be easier. When you are done with this aspect of editing, reformat your text to draw everything back together.

18

"How Can This Be a Run-On or a Comma Splice? It's Not Even Long."

If you have a tendency to write run-on sentences or comma splices, take comfort in the fact that you are not alone. They are two of the most frequently occurring writing errors.

A *run-on sentence* occurs when two word groups that can be sentences (*independent clauses*) stand together without any separation. A *comma splice* occurs when two word groups that can be sentences (independent clauses) stand together with only a comma between them.

Here are two word groups that can be sentences (independent clauses):

Independent clause: Charleston Harbor is a fascinating place to visit

Independent clause: many historical attractions are there

A *run-on sentence* is created when these independent clauses are not separated:

Run-on sentence: Charleston Harbor is a fascinating place to visit many historical attractions are there.

A *comma splice* is created when two independent clauses are separated by nothing more than a comma:

Comma splice: Charleston Harbor is a fascinating place to visit, many historical attractions are there.

121

Run-on sentences and comma splices are a problem because they blur the points where sentences begin and end. To eliminate run-on sentences and comma splices, the independent clauses can be separated in one of three ways, as follows:

1. **With a comma and *coordinating conjunction* (*and, but, or, nor, for, so, yet*)**

   Charleston Harbor is a fascinating place to visit, for many historical attractions are there.

2. **With a semicolon (;)**

   Charleston Harbor is a fascinating place to visit; many historical attractions are there.

3. **With a period and a capital letter**

   Charleston Harbor is a fascinating place to visit. Many historical attractions are there.

The rest of this chapter describes ways to find run-on sentences and comma splices in your writing.

STUDY SENTENCES INDIVIDUALLY

Study each of your sentences separately. Place one finger of your left hand under the capital letter and one finger of your right hand under the period, question mark, or exclamation point. Then identify the number of independent clauses (word groups that can stand as sentences) between your fingers. If you have one, the sentence is fine. If you have two or more, look to see what is separating the clauses. If a semicolon separates the independent clauses, the sentence is fine; if a comma and coordinating conjunction (*and, but, or, nor, for, so, yet*) separate the independent clauses, the sentence is fine. However, if nothing separates the independent clauses, or if only a comma without a coordinating conjunction separates the independent clauses, then you have a problem.

Move through your whole draft this way checking for and eliminating run-ons and comma splices. Although time-consuming, this procedure is very effective.

UNDERLINE RUN-ON AND COMMA SPLICE WARNING WORDS

When you edit for run-ons and comma splices, pay special attention to these words because they often begin independent clauses (word groups that can be sentences):

he	however	then	moreover	nevertheless
she	therefore	thus	furthermore	similarly
it	hence	finally	consequently	next
they	as a result	in addition	on the contrary	for example

Read over your draft and underline any of these warning words that appear. Then check to see what is on *both sides* of each underlined word. If—and only if—an independent clause is on *both sides,* place a semicolon (not a comma) before the warning word.

Forget about Long and Short

Many people think that a long sentence is sure to be a run-on or comma splice. Similarly, they think that a short sentence cannot possibly be one. This thinking is mistaken, for length is not a factor. The only factor is how independent clauses are separated, so during this phase of editing forget about how long or short your sentences are.

Use a Computer

The strategies that follow will help you locate run-on sentences and comma splices using computer technology.

Search for Warning Words. Use the search function to find all the run-on warning words (see page 122). Once these words are identified, check for independent clauses on both sides of these words. Wherever you find independent clauses on *both sides* of a warning word, be sure you have a semicolon before the word.

Isolate Sentences. Press the enter key before every capital letter marking the beginning of a sentence to reformat your paper into a list. This will make it easier to study sentences individually, following the procedure described on page 122. After finding and eliminating run-ons and comma splices, reformat your text to bring everything back together.

19

"I/ME, SHE/HER, HE/HIM, THEY/THEM, WE/US, WHO/WHOM— WHAT'S THE DIFFERENCE?"

There you are writing along merrily, and then it happens—you have to use a pronoun and you are not sure which one is correct: Did the police officer issue the warning to Lee and me or to Lee and I? "Lee and me; no, it's Lee and I; no, wait, Lee and me." Ah, what the heck—you pick one and hope for the best.

Writers often stumble over pronouns, but the procedures in this chapter can help.

CROSS OUT EVERYTHING IN THE PHRASE BUT THE PRONOUN

When a pronoun is joined with a noun, you may be unsure which pronoun to use. Is it "Luis and I" or "Luis and me"? Is it "the girls and us" or "the girls and we"? To decide, cross out everything in the phrase but the pronoun and read what is left:

~~My brothers and~~ I saw the movie six times.

~~My brothers and~~ me saw the movie six times.

With everything but the pronoun crossed out, you can tell that the correct choice is *I*:

My brothers and I saw the movie six times.

Here is another example:

> Dr. Cohen lent ~~Maria and~~ I a copy of the book.
> Dr. Cohen lent ~~Maria and~~ me a copy of the book.

With everything but the pronoun crossed out, you can tell that the correct choice is *me:*

> Dr. Cohen lent Maria and me a copy of the book.

CROSS OUT WORDS THAT RENAME

Sometimes words follow a pronoun and rename it. The words that rename are called *appositives.*

We baseball players:	<u>Baseball players</u> follows the pronoun and renames it.
Us sophomores:	<u>Sophomores</u> follows the pronoun and renames it.
You sports fans:	<u>Sports fans</u> follows the pronoun and renames it.

To choose the correct pronoun, cross out the words that rename (the appositives):

> We ~~spectators~~ jumped to our feet and cheered when the band took the field.
> Us ~~spectators~~ jumped to our feet and cheered when the band took the field.

With the appositive crossed out, the correct choice is clear:

> We spectators jumped to our feet and cheered when the band took the field.

Here is another example:

> Loud rock music can be irritating to we ~~older folks.~~
> Loud rock music can be irritating to us ~~older folks.~~

With the appositive crossed out, the correct choice is clear:

> Loud rock music can be irritating to us older folks.

Add the Missing Words in Comparisons

Which is it: "Bev is a better foul shooter than I" or "Bev is a better foul shooter than me"? To find out, add the unstated comparison word:

Bev is a better foul shooter than I am.

Bev is a better foul shooter than me am.

With the missing word added, you can tell that the correct pronoun is *I:*

Bev is a better foul shooter than I.

Here is another example:

John Grisham's new novel interested Miguel as much as I.

John Grisham's new novel interested Miguel as much as me.

To decide on the correct pronoun, add the missing words:

John Grisham's new novel interested Miguel as much as it interested I.

John Grisham's new novel interested Miguel as much as it interested me.

With the missing comparison words added, you can tell that the correct pronoun is *me.*

Circle *They, Their,* and *Them,* and Draw an Arrow to the Nouns They Refer To

They, their, and *them* refer to plural nouns:

All students should bring (their) notebooks to the next class; if (they) forget (them), class participation will prove difficult.

A problem occurs when *they, their,* or *them* is used to refer to a singular noun:

A person who cares about the environment will recycle. (They) will also avoid using Styrofoam and plastic.

In the previous sentence the plural *they* refers to the singular *person,* creating a problem called *lack of agreement.* To eliminate the problem, make the pronoun and noun agree in one of these two ways:

Singular noun
and pronoun: A person who cares about the environment will recycle. (He or she) will also avoid using Styrofoam and plastic.

Plural noun
and pronoun: People who care about the environment will recycle. (They) will also avoid using Styrofoam and plastic.

One way to ensure agreement is to circle *they, their,* and *them* and then draw arrows to the nouns referred to. Be sure each of these pronouns refers to a plural noun. If it does not, make the noun plural or change the pronoun to a singular form.

PAY SPECIAL ATTENTION TO EVERYBODY, EVERYONE, EVERYTHING, SOMEBODY, SOMEONE, SOMETHING, ANYBODY, ANYONE, AND ANYTHING

In formal usage, these nine words (called *indefinite pronouns*) are singular (*-body, -one,* and *-thing* at the end can help you remember this). Thus, pronouns that refer to these words should also be singular if you are writing for an audience that expects formal usage. Here are some examples:

Everybody should remember his or her admission forms when reporting to orientation.

Someone left his or her coat in the auditorium.

Anybody who wants to bring his or her family may do so.

Be sure to put everything in its place.

When you edit, look for these nine words. If you find one, look to see if a pronoun refers to it. If so, be sure that the pronoun is singular. Do not rely on the sound of the sentence because the plural pronoun may sound fine since it is often used in informal spoken English.

CIRCLE WHO AND WHOM AND UNDERLINE THE REST OF THE CLAUSE

Writers often have trouble choosing between *who* and *whom.* To solve the problem, circle *who* or *whom* and underline the rest of the *clause* (word group with a subject and verb). If the circled word acts as a subject, use *who*. If it is the object, use *whom*. Here are some examples:

> Hippocrates, (who or whom?) lived about 400 B.C., is called the "Father of Medicine."

Choose *who* because it is the subject of the verb *lived*.

> Hippocrates, who lived about 400 B.C., is called the "Father of Medicine."

> I attended the lecture by the Holocaust survivor (who or whom?) the community invited to speak.

Choose *whom* because it is the object of the verb *invited*.

> I attended the lecture by the Holocaust survivor whom the community invited to speak.

CIRCLE *YOU*

The pronoun *you* addresses the reader; if it is used to refer to someone other than the reader, the result is a problem called *person shift.* To avoid this problem, circle *you* and draw an arrow to the word it refers to. If this word names someone other than the reader, replace *you* with the correct pronoun. Here is an example:

> Distance runners must train religiously. (You) cannot compete successfully if (you) run only on weekends.

Now here is the corrected version:

> Distance runners must train religiously. (They) cannot compete successfully if (they) run only on weekends.

UNDERLINE *IT* AND *THEY* TO AVOID UNSTATED REFERENCE

Underline *it* and *they* and then check that you have supplied a noun for each of these words to refer to. Otherwise, you will have a problem called *unstated reference.*

Unstated reference: Charlie is a very curious child. Because of it, he asks questions all the time.

Explanation:	*It* cannot refer to *curious* because *curious* is a modifier, not a noun. The reference is meant to be *curiosity*, but that word is not stated.
Correction:	Charlie is a very curious child. Because of his curiosity, he asks questions all the time.
Unstated reference:	When I went to the unemployment office, <u>they</u> told me that some construction jobs were available.
Explanation:	There is no stated noun for *they* to refer to.
Correction:	When I went to the unemployment office, the employment counselor told me that some construction jobs were available.

WATCH OUT FOR UNCLEAR REFERENCE

When a pronoun can refer to more than one noun, the reader cannot tell what the writer means, creating a problem called *unclear reference.*

Unclear reference:	Dad was in the garage with Brian when he heard the telephone ring.
Explanation:	Because of unclear reference, the reader can't tell whether Dad or Brian heard the phone.
Correction:	Dad was in the garage with Brian when Brian heard the telephone ring.

BE CAREFUL OF *THIS* AND *WHICH*

To avoid confusion, make sure that *this* and *which* refer to specific nouns.

Confusing:	When people send e-mail, they expect an immediate response, whereas when they send a traditional memo, they do not expect a quick reply. <u>This</u> interests communications specialists. (What interests communication specialists: people expecting an immediate response, people not expecting a quick reply, or the difference in expectations?)
Better:	When people send e-mail, they expect an immediate response, whereas when they send a traditional memo, they do not expect a quick reply. <u>This difference</u> interests communications specialists.

Confusing: I told my supervisor that I could not work on Saturday, <u>which</u> upset my coworkers. (What upset the coworkers: the fact that the writer could not work or the fact that the supervisor was told?)

Better: My coworkers were annoyed because I told my supervisor that I could not work on Saturday.

USE A COMPUTER

The search or find function can help you check your use of some pronouns. First, use it to locate these pronouns in your draft: *they, their, them.* Then check to be sure that you have plural nouns for these words to refer to. Also, check to be sure *they* has a stated noun to refer to.

Next, locate every use of *everyone, everybody, everything, someone, somebody, something, anyone, anybody,* and *anything.* Check to see if a pronoun refers to each of these words. If so, use the singular form for formal usage.

Now locate every use of *who* and *whom.* If the word is used as a subject, use *who;* if it is used as an object, use *whom.*

Then locate every use of *you.* See if you need to change this pronoun because it is not really referring to the reader. Finally, locate *which* and *this* and be sure they refer to specific nouns.

20

"How Do I Know Which Verb Form to Use?"

Choosing the right verb can be tricky at times, but most of the problems arise in just a few special instances. Strategies for dealing with these instances are discussed in this chapter.

Cross Out Phrases before the Verb

A phrase before the verb can trick you into choosing the wrong verb form. Consider this sentence:

The stack of books (is or are?) about to fall.

Is it *The stack is* or *The books are*? To decide, cross out the phrase *of books* to get:

The stack ~~of books~~ is about to fall.

Phrases before the verb often begin with one of these words (called *prepositions*):

about	before	inside	over
above	between	into	through
across	by	like	to

Continued

after	during	near	toward
among	for	next	under
around	from	of	up
at	in	on	with

When in doubt about the correct verb form, cross out phrases beginning with one of these words. Here are some examples:

The container of old dishes (<u>is</u> or <u>are</u>?) on the landing.

The container ~~of old dishes~~ (<u>is</u> or <u>are</u>?) on the landing.

The container of old dishes is on the landing.

The herd of steers (<u>graze</u> or <u>grazes</u>?) contentedly.

The herd ~~of steers~~ (<u>graze</u> or <u>grazes</u>?) contentedly.

The herd of steers grazes contentedly.

The characteristics of the German shepherd (<u>make</u> or <u>makes</u>?) him a suitable show dog.

The characteristics ~~of the German shepherd~~ (<u>make</u> or <u>makes</u>?) him a suitable show dog.

The characteristics of the German shepherd make him a suitable show dog.

REWRITE QUESTIONS

Choosing the correct verb is tricky in sentences that ask questions, because the verb comes before the subject. Verb choice is easier, however, if you rewrite the sentence so it is no longer a question. Here is an example:

Sentence with question:	(<u>Have</u> or <u>has</u>?) the students finished taking exams?
Sentence rewritten:	The students have finished taking exams.
Sentence with question and correct verb:	Have the students finished taking exams?

REWRITE SENTENCES BEGINNING WITH *HERE* AND *THERE*

When a sentence begins with *here* or *there,* the verb comes before the subject, which makes verb choice a little tricky. When uncertain, rewrite the sentence putting the subject before the verb. The correct choice should be easier that way.

Sentence with *here:*   Here (<u>is</u> or <u>are</u>?) the important papers you asked for.

Sentence rewritten: The important papers you asked for are here.

Sentence with *here* and correct verb: Here are the important papers you asked for.

Sentence with *there:*   There (<u>was</u> or <u>were</u>?) an excellent dance band playing at the wedding reception.

Sentence rewritten: An excellent dance band was playing at the wedding reception.

Sentence with *there* and correct verb: There was an excellent dance band playing at the wedding reception.

WATCH OUT FOR SUBJECTS JOINED BY *OR* AND *EITHER/OR*

Whether subjects joined by *or* and *either/or* (called *compound subjects*) take a singular or plural verb depends on what subjects are joined.

1. **If both subjects are singular, use a singular verb.**

   (Joyce) or (Kico) <u>expects</u> to pick me up for the concert.

   Either the (steak) or the (veal roast) <u>is</u> on sale at the market.

2. **If both subjects are plural, use a plural verb.**

   The (boxes) or the (fishing poles) <u>are</u> behind the door.

   Either the (scouts) or their leaders <u>visit</u> the elderly every week.

3. **If one subject is singular and the other is plural, place the plural subject second and use a plural verb.**

   The (gardenia) or the (roses) <u>make</u> a lovely centerpiece.

   Either my (sister) or my (brothers) <u>cook</u> Thanksgiving dinner each year.

CIRCLE *EACH, EITHER, NEITHER, ONE, NONE, ANYONE, ANYBODY, ANYTHING, EVERYONE, EVERYBODY, EVERYTHING, SOMEONE, SOMEBODY,* AND *SOMETHING*

These words are *indefinite pronouns,* and in formal usage they take singular verbs—even though the sense of the sentence suggests that a plural verb is logical. To check for the correct verb when you have used one of these words as the subject of a sentence, circle the word and draw an arrow to the verb. Then check that verb to be sure it is singular.

(Each) of the students wants (not <u>want</u>) to have the test on Friday so the weekend is more relaxing.

(One) of the first museums was (not <u>were</u>) Altes Museum in Berlin.

(Either) of these vacation plans meets (not <u>meet</u>) your needs.

(Neither) of these paintings suits (not <u>suit</u>) my taste.

(None) of Lin's excuses is (not <u>are</u>) believable.

Do not rely on the sound of the sentence because the plural verb may sound fine, and the singular verb may sound a little off. This is because the plural verb is often used in informal speech and writing. Nonetheless, use the singular verb for strict grammatical correctness in formal usage.

LISTEN TO YOUR VERB TENSES

Tense means time. Many verbs change their form to show different tenses (times):

Present tense (time):	Today I <u>walk</u> two miles for exercise.
Past tense (time):	Yesterday I <u>walked</u> two miles for exercise.
Future tense (time):	Tomorrow I <u>will walk</u> two miles for exercise.

Sometimes a change in verb tense is necessary to show a change in time, but if you change tense inappropriately, you create a problem called *tense shift*.

Appropriate change in tense from present to past:	I <u>recall</u> that April Fools' Day <u>began</u> in France.
Problem tense shift from present to past:	After I <u>finish</u> my work, I <u>watched</u> a movie.

Read your draft out loud and listen to your verb tenses. You are likely to hear problem tense shifts.

CHAPTER

21

"I'm Unsure about Using Modifiers."

A *modifier* is a word or phrase that describes. For example, consider this sentence:

Because of the terrible accident, traffic moved slowly.

Because *terrible* describes *accident*, *terrible* is a modifier; because *slowly* describes *moved*, *slowly* is a modifier. Modifiers take different forms in different grammatical settings. If those forms give you some trouble, the suggestions in this chapter can help.

Draw an Arrow from the Modifier to the Word Described

Which sentence is correct?

The party ended so <u>abruptly</u> that no one had a chance to eat.

The party ended so <u>abrupt</u> that no one had a chance to eat.

If you are unsure, you may have trouble knowing when to use adjectives and when to use adverbs. An *adjective* describes a noun or pronoun, and an *adverb* describes a verb or other modifier. Frequently, the adverb form ends in *-ly* and the adjective form does not.

135

Adjectives	Adverbs
brief	briefly
swift	swiftly
loud	loudly
clear	clearly

When in doubt, draw an arrow from the modifier to the word it describes. If the arrow is drawn to a noun or pronoun, then use the adjective form. If the arrow is drawn to a verb or modifier, then use the adverb form. Here is an example.

Is it *quick* or *quickly* in this sentence?

Diane mowed the lawn (quick or quickly?) so she could leave with her friends.

To decide, draw an arrow from the modifier to the word described. If the word described is a noun or a pronoun, use the adjective; if it is a verb or another modifier, use the adverb (which often ends in *-ly*).

Diane mowed the lawn (quick or quickly?) so she could leave with her friends.

Now you can tell that *quickly* is called for because a verb is described:

Diane mowed the lawn quickly so she could leave with her friends.

Here are some more examples:

David was (absolute or absolutely?) sure of the answer.

David was absolutely sure of the answer. (A modifier is described, so the adverb is used.)

The ancient Egyptians thought of the soul as a bird that could fly around (easy or easily?)

The ancient Egyptians thought of the soul as a bird that could fly around easily. (A verb is described, so the adverb is used.)

Chris is (happy or happily?) that he was promoted after only one month on the job.

Chris is happy that he was promoted after only one month on the job. (A noun is described, so the adjective is used.)

REMEMBER THAT *GOOD* IS AN ADJECTIVE AND *WELL* IS AN ADVERB—WITH ONE CAUTION AND ONE EXCEPTION

Good is an adjective; it describes nouns and pronouns:

The good news is that I got the job.

Well is an adverb; it describes verbs and modifiers:

After 10 years of lessons, Maxine plays the piano well.

Now here's the caution: After verbs like *taste, seem, appear,* and *look,* use *good* because the noun or pronoun before the verb is being described.

The meat tastes good, even though it is overcooked.

Claudia looks good, although she just had surgery.

The restaurant seems good, so let's eat here.

Now here's the exception: *Well* is used as an adjective to mean "in good health."

After six brownies and a bottle of soda, the child did not feel well.

EACH TIME YOU USE *MORE* OR *MOST,* CHECK TO BE SURE YOU HAVE NOT USED AN *-ER* OR *-EST* FORM

Yes: I like tacos <u>better</u> than nachos.

No: I like tacos <u>more better</u> than nachos.

Yes: The Sahara Desert is the world's <u>hottest</u> region in summer.

No: The Sahara Desert is the world's <u>most hottest</u> region in summer.

Yes: The Sahara Desert is <u>bigger</u> than the United States.

No: The Sahara Desert is <u>more bigger</u> than the United States.

Yes: The <u>rainiest</u> place on earth is Mount Waialeale, in Hawaii.

No: The <u>most rainiest</u> place on earth is Mount Waialeale, in Hawaii.

CHECK EVERY SENTENCE THAT OPENS WITH AN *-ING* OR *-ED* VERB FORM

An *-ing* or *-ed* verb form (called a *participle)* can be used as an adjective:

Whistling, Carolyn strolled through the park.

Whistling is a verb form that is used as an adjective to describe *Carolyn.*

Living only two or three years, lizards have a short life span.

Living is a verb form used as an adjective to describe *lizards.*

When an *-ing* or *-ed* form opens a sentence, it must be followed by the word that the form describes. Otherwise, the result will be a *dangling modifier.* Dangling modifiers can create some pretty silly sentences:

Dangling modifier: While making the coffee, the toast burned. (This sentence says that the toast made the coffee.)

Correction: While making the coffee, I burned the toast. (The opening *-ing* verb form is followed by a word it can sensibly describe.)

Dangling modifier: Exhausted from work, a nap was needed. (This sentence says that the nap was exhausted.)

Correction: Exhausted from work, Lucy needed a nap. (The opening *-ed* verb form is followed by a word it can logically describe.)

If you are in the habit of writing dangling modifiers, check every opening *-ing* and *-ed* verb form to be sure it is closely followed by a word it can sensibly describe.

MOVE MODIFIERS NEAR THE WORDS THEY DESCRIBE

If a modifier is too far from the word it describes, the result is a *misplaced modifier.* A misplaced modifier can create a silly sentence:

Misplaced modifier: Lee bought a bicycle from a neighbor with a flat tire. (The sentence says that the neighbor had a flat tire.)

Correction: Lee bought a bicycle with a flat tire from a neighbor. (The modifier has been moved closer to the word it describes.)

22

"Why Can't I Place a Comma Wherever I Pause?"

Placing commas wherever you pause is an unreliable method of punctuating: sometimes it works and sometimes it doesn't. Your best bet is to learn the rules. Editing strategies are given in this chapter to help you follow these common comma rules:

1. Use a comma after an introductory element.

2. Use a comma before a coordinating conjunction that joins independent clauses.

3. Use a comma to separate items in a series.

4. Use a comma to set off nonessential sentence elements.

For other important comma rules, consult a grammar handbook.

Find the Subject and Look in Front of It (to Help You Place Commas after Introductory Elements)

Most of the time, anything that comes before the subject of a sentence (that is, any *introductory element*) is set off with a comma. It does not matter whether the material is one word, a phrase, or a clause. Thus, once you identify the subject of a sentence, you can look in front of it. If there are any words there, follow them with a comma, like this:

Word before
the subject:

subject

Surprisingly, <u>the heart of a whale</u> beats only nine times a minute.

Phrase before
the subject:

subject

In medieval Japan, <u>fashionable women</u> blackened their teeth to enhance their appearance.

Clause before
the subject:

subject

Although Albert Einstein developed the theory of relativity, <u>he</u> failed his first college entrance exam.

CIRCLE *AND, BUT, OR, NOR, FOR, SO, YET* AND LOOK LEFT AND RIGHT (TO HELP YOU USE COMMAS BEFORE COORDINATING CONJUNCTIONS THAT JOIN INDEPENDENT CLAUSES)

If a word group that can stand as a sentence (an *independent clause*) appears on *both sides* of *and, but, or, nor, for, so, yet (coordinating conjunctions),* you should place a comma before the conjunction.

To apply this rule, circle every coordinating conjunction; then look left and right. If an independent clause appears on both sides, place a comma before the conjunction.

Use comma:

independent clause

[I enjoy reading Stephen King novels], (but) [I do not enjoy

independent clause

watching horror movies.]

Use comma:

independent clause

[The Centers for Disease Control predicts a flu outbreak], (so) [I plan

independent clause

to get a flu shot.]

Use comma:

independent clause   independent clause

[Fish can distinguish colors], (and) [they actually prefer some colors over others.]

Do not
use comma:

not a clause

The owl cannot move its eyes (but) [can turn its head around.]

Do not
use comma:

not a clause

The car accelerated quickly (and) [turned left.]

Do not
use comma:

not a clause

You can leave with me now (or) [wait until later.]

Look for Series (to help You Separate Items in a Series)

A *series* is three or more words, phrases, or clauses. Separate the items in a series with commas.

Words in a series:	This restaurant specializes in <u>pasta</u>, <u>steak</u>, <u>salads</u>, and <u>seafood.</u>
Phrases in a series:	Recycling centers have been established <u>at the government center</u>, <u>behind the high school</u>, and <u>at the baseball fields</u>.
Clauses in a series:	<u>The manager lowered prices</u>, <u>the sales staff tried to be more helpful</u>, and <u>the owner remodeled the store</u>.

Identify Nonessential Elements (to Help You Set Off Nonessential Elements)

A *nonessential element* can be removed without changing the meaning of the sentence. Identify nonessential elements and set them off with commas. In the following sentences, the nonessential elements are underscored as a study aid.

Nonessential word:	The president at the time, Carter, worked to achieve the Egyptian-Israeli peace agreement.
Nonessential word:	The governor, <u>surprisingly</u>, opposed the balanced-budget amendment.
Nonessential phrase:	You can, <u>of course</u>, join us for dinner.
Nonessential phrase:	The crime rate, <u>according to the newspaper</u>, has not increased this year.
Nonessential clause:	Very few people understand how the election process works, <u>if you ask me</u>.
Nonessential clause:	Karen Carpenter, <u>who died of anorexia nervosa</u>, was a talented performer.

23

"What Do I Do If I Want to Quote Somebody?"

From time to time, you will want to reproduce the words someone has spoken or written: Those words may advance a story; they may add vividness; they may lend insight into character; or they may provide support for an idea. No matter what motivates you to do so, when you quote someone, you are obligated to get it right. That means you must reproduce the words *exactly* as they were spoken or written, and it means you must follow the relevant punctuation and capitalization rules—the ones given in this chapter.

Punctuate and Capitalize According to Where in the Sentence the Quotation Occurs

If your quotation comes *after* the statement of who spoke, model this form:

Eli reminded us, "Put out the campfire before retiring."

If your quotation comes *before* the statement of who spoke, model this form:

"Put out the campfire before retiring," Eli reminded us.

DETERMINE WHETHER THE QUOTATION OR THE ENTIRE SENTENCE ASKS A QUESTION

When the quotation asks a question, model one of these forms:

The reporter asked Senator McEwin, "Did you vote for the trade bill?"

"Did you vote for the trade bill?" the reporter asked Senator McEwin.

When the entire sentence asks a question, model this form:

Did the newspaper really say, "The president of the school board plans to resign"? (The question mark appears outside the quotation mark.)

REPRODUCE A PERSON'S THOUGHTS AS A QUOTATION

A person's thoughts are treated like spoken words, especially when a story is being told. Here is an example:

Julia thought, "It's time I made a change in my life."

BE SURE YOU REALLY HAVE EXACT WORDS

Before using quotation marks, be sure you are reproducing someone's exact words.

Use quotation marks (exact words):	The police officer said, "Move your car."
Do not use quotation marks (not exact words):	The police officer said that you should move your car.

24

"I Have Trouble with Apostrophes."

Apostrophes have two main functions: They are used in contractions to take the place of missing letters, and they signal possession. Some people think apostrophes have a third function: to drive them crazy. Apostrophes *can* be pesky, so if you are unsure how to use them, try the techniques presented in this chapter.

Identify the Missing Letter(s) in a Contraction

A *contraction* is formed by taking two words, dropping one or more letters, and joining the two words into one. In contractions, discover which letter or letters are missing, and place the apostrophe at the site of the missing letter(s). For example, the contraction form of *did not* is *didn't*. Because the *o* is left out of *not*, the apostrophe is placed between the *n* and the *t*. Here are some more examples:

have + not = haven't (apostrophe at site of missing *o*)

we + will = we'll (apostrophe at site of missing *wi*)

it + is = it's (apostrophe at site of missing *i*)

✔ NOTE: *The contraction form of will not is the unusual won't.*

Use *It's* Only When You Can Substitute *It Is* or *It Has*

1. **It's is the contraction form of *it is* or *it has*.**

    It's time for a change of leadership in this state.
    (It is time for a change of leadership in this state.)

    It's been 10 years since I smoked a cigarette.
    (It has been 10 years since I smoked a cigarette.)

2. **Its is a possessive form; it shows ownership and cannot be substituted for *it is* or *it has*.**

    Yes: The river overflowed its banks. (*Its* shows ownership.)

    No: Its too late to turn back now.

    Yes: It's too late to turn back now. (*It's* here means *it is*.)

Avoid Contractions

No law says that you must use contractions. If you are unsure where to place the apostrophe, use the two-word form instead of the contraction.

For Possessive Forms, Ask Two Questions

Apostrophes are used with nouns to show possession. To determine how to use the apostrophe, ask, "Does the noun end in *s?*"

1. **If the noun *does not* end in *s*, add an apostrophe and an *s*, like this:**

    President + 's = President's

    The President's Council on Aging reports an increase in homelessness among the elderly.

    children + 's = children's

    Children's toys cost more money than they are worth.

2. **If the noun ends in *s*, ask, "Is the noun singular or plural?"**

    a.   If the noun is singular, add an apostrophe and an *s*, like this:

    Delores + 's = Delores's

Delores's new car was hit in the parking lot.

bus + 's = bus's

The bus's brakes jammed, causing a minor accident.

b. If the noun is plural, add an apostrophe, like this:

shoes + ' = shoes'

All the shoes' laces are too long.

mayors + ' = mayors'

The three mayors' mutual aid agreement will yield economic benefits.

USE A COMPUTER

If you use your computer's spell check, remember that many programs do not check apostrophes in contractions, so misspellings such as "cant" will not be noted.

25

"I CAN'T SPELL."

There's good news and bad news. First the bad news: Misspelled words are a problem because they lead the reader to think you are not capable. Now the good news: Lots of capable people do not spell well, but they have learned ways to solve their spelling problem. You, too, can eliminate misspellings with the techniques in this chapter.

WHEN IN DOUBT, CHECK IT OUT

When it comes to using a dictionary, we all get lazy. Still, the only surefire way to check a spelling is to look up the word. If you have the slightest suspicion that a word is misspelled, check the dictionary.

BUY TWO DICTIONARIES

So looking words up is as convenient as possible, buy two dictionaries: a hardback collegiate dictionary to keep on your writing desk and a fat paperback to carry with you. You are more likely to look up a word if you have a dictionary at hand and do not have to get up and walk somewhere.

USE A SPELLING DICTIONARY

Spelling dictionaries, available in most drugstores and bookstores, reference frequently misspelled words. They provide spellings without definitions, so these volumes are thin, which makes them convenient to carry around. If you must look up words often, a spelling dictionary may prove less cumbersome than a standard dictionary.

USE A POCKET SPELL CHECKER

Pocket spell checkers are electronic gadgets about the size of some calculators. They can be expensive, but if you are more inclined to check spellings with an electronic gizmo than with a dictionary, they are worth the money.

LEARN CORRECT PRONUNCIATIONS

Sometimes people misspell because they pronounce a word incorrectly. For example, *February* may be misspelled if it is pronounced "Feb · u · ary"; *preventive* may be misspelled if it is pronounced "pre · ven · ta · tive."

BREAK A WORD INTO PARTS

When a word is composed of identifiable parts, spell the word out part by part. Words like the following may be more manageable when spelled out part by part:

under · stand · able	with · hold	arm · chair
room · mate	kinder · garten	dis · ease
comfort · able	lone · liness	over · coat

BREAK A WORD INTO SYLLABLES

Some words are more easily spelled if you go syllable by syllable. Words of three or more syllables are often better handled this way.

or · gan · i · za · tion	cit · i · zen	mon · u · men · tal
Jan · u · ar · y	in · vi · ta · tion	hos · pi · tal
in · di · vis · i · ble	con · ver · sa · tion	pro · ba · bly

LOOK FOR PREFIXES

When a *prefix* (word beginning) is added to a word, the spelling of the base word will probably not change.

mis · take	dis · satisfaction	mis · spell
un · nerve	un · necessary	pre · pare
mis · inform	inter · related	pre · record

USE MEMORY TRICKS

Think of tricks to help you spell words. For example, the word *instrument* contains *strum,* and you strum a guitar, which is an instrument. Actors in a *tragedy* often *rage* at each other.

Memory tricks can be particularly helpful for pairs of words that are often mistaken for each other. You may find some of the following tricks to your liking, and you may want to make up tricks for other pairs of words that you confuse.

1. **advice/advise**

   a. *Advice* means "a suggestion."

      Joel's <u>advice</u> proved sound.

   b. *Advise* means "to give advice."

      Yvette is the best person to <u>advise</u> you.

   ✔ *MEMORY TRICK: A person with a <u>vice</u> needs ad<u>vice</u>.*

2. **affect/effect**

   a. *Affect* means "to influence."

      The drought will <u>affect</u> the economy for years to come.

b. *Effect* means "result."

The <u>effects</u> of the drought are devastating.

✔ *MEMORY TRICK: The first syllable of <u>effect</u> rhymes with the first syllable of <u>result</u>.*

3. **among/between**

a. *Among* is used for more than two.

Divide the candy <u>among</u> the four children.

b. *Between* is used for two.

The difference <u>between</u> the ages of Phil and Carlos is not important.

✔ *MEMORY TRICK: Can you fit anything <u>between</u> the <u>two e's</u> in the last syllable of <u>between?</u>*

4. **beside/besides**

a. *Beside* means "alongside of."

I parked the van <u>beside</u> the Corvette.

b. *Besides* means "in addition to."

<u>Besides</u> good soil, the plants need water.

✔ *MEMORY TRICK: The final <u>s</u> in <u>besides</u> is "in addition to" the first <u>s.</u>*

5. **fewer/less**

a. *Fewer* is for things that can be counted.

<u>Fewer</u> people voted in this election than in the last one.

b. *Less* is used for things that cannot be counted.

People who exercise regularly experience <u>less</u> stress than those who do not.

✔ *MEMORY TRICK: Think of <u>countless. Less</u> is used for things that cannot be counted.*

6. **then/than**

a. *Then* refers to a certain time.

The trumpets blared; <u>then</u> the cymbals crashed.

b. *Than* is used to compare.

I like small classes better <u>than</u> large lectures.

✔ *MEMORY TRICK: Think of the <u>e</u> in <u>then</u> and <u>time;</u> think of the <u>a</u> in <u>than</u> and <u>compare.</u>*

LEARN THE HOMOPHONES

Homophones sound alike, but they are spelled and used differently. Learn the following homophones and any others that give you trouble.

1. **all ready/already**

   a. *All ready* means "all set."

      By three o'clock, the family was <u>all ready</u> to leave for Virginia Beach.

   b. *Already* means "by this time."

      We are <u>already</u> an hour behind schedule, and we haven't begun the trip yet.

2. **its/it's**

   a. *Its* shows ownership.

      The car hit a pothole and broke <u>its</u> axle.

   b. *It's* is the contraction form of "it is" or "it has."

      <u>It's</u> too late to say you are sorry.

      <u>It's</u> been 10 years since graduation.

3. **passed/past**

   a. *Passed* means "went by" or "handed."

      Katie <u>passed</u> the potatoes to Earvin.

      The shooting star <u>passed</u> overhead at nine o'clock.

   b. *Past* refers to previous time. It also means "by."

      I have learned from <u>past</u> experience not to trust Jerry.

      When I drove <u>past</u> the house, no one was home.

4. **principal/principle**

   a. *Principal* means "main" or "most important." It is also the school official.

      The <u>principal</u> roadblock to peace is the personalities of the country's leaders.

      The high school <u>principal</u> favors a dress code.

    b.   *Principle* is a truth or standard.

       The <u>principles</u> of world economics are studied in this course.

5. **there/their/they're**

    a.   *There* refers to direction or place. It is also opens sentences.

       Place the vase of flowers <u>there</u> on the coffee table.

       <u>There</u> is a surprise for you in the kitchen.

    b.   *Their* shows ownership.

       The students revised <u>their</u> drafts in the computer lab.

    c.   *They're* is the contraction form of "they are."

       Do not sit Lee and Dana next to each other; <u>they're</u> not getting along.

6. **threw/through**

    a.   *Threw* is the past tense of *throw.*

       The shortstop <u>threw</u> the ball to the pitcher.

    b.   *Through* means "in one side and out the other" or "finished."

       I had trouble getting the thread <u>through</u> the needle.

       My morning biology class is not <u>through</u> until 11:00 o'clock.

7. **to/too/two**

    a.   *To* means "toward." It is also used with a verb to form the *infinitive.*

       Liza usually walks <u>to</u> school.

       Eric is learning how <u>to</u> play the violin.

    b.   *Too* means "excessively" or "also."

       I find it <u>too</u> hot in this building.

       Juanita works in the library, and she tutors math <u>too</u>.

    c.   *Two* is the number.

       <u>Two</u> weeks ago, I bought a new car.

8. **your/you're**

    a.   *Your* shows ownership.

       You left <u>your</u> keys in the car.

    b.   *You're* is the contraction form of "you are."

       If <u>you're</u> leaving now, please take me with you.

UNDERLINE WORDS TO CHECK LATER

When you write a word while drafting or revising, you may have a sense that it is spelled wrong. Yet, looking the word up at that point is undesirable because it interrupts the drafting or revising momentum. To solve this problem, underline every word whose spelling you are unsure of as you write it. Then you have a visual reminder to look up the word later, when it is more convenient.

KEEP A SPELLING LIST

Look up the words you misspell and add the words, correctly spelled, to a list for study. Each day, study the list and memorize another word or two in an effort to increase the number of words you can spell.

USE A COMPUTER

Spell checkers test every word you have written against the words in the dictionary in the computer's memory. If a word is not recognized, the spell checker will offer alternative spellings. If the spell checker comes across a typing error, it may be baffled if nothing in its memory comes close to the spelling. In this case, it will not know what to suggest as a correct spelling. Also, homophones (soundalikes) are untouched by spell checkers, so the confusion of something like *there, their, they're* will not be resolved. Finally, resist the temptation to accept automatically the first spelling offered by a spell checker, as it may not be the one you should use. Despite these limitations, spell checkers can be helpful to people with chronic spelling problems.

V

WRITING PRACTICE

The writing tasks in the next chapter give you opportunities to practice so you can continue to improve. If you get stuck along the way, refer to the appropriate chapters of this book for troubleshooting suggestions.

26

IDEAS FOR WRITING

1. The student services division of your university plans to publish a handbook for incoming freshmen to familiarize them with some of the most common procedures on campus. As a student employee in student services, you have been asked to contribute to the handbook by writing an essay that explains how to do one of the following:

    a. Get a student I.D.

    b. Register for courses.

    c. Select a suitable advisor.

    d. Rush a fraternity or sorority.

    e. Manage stress.

    f. Prepare for final examinations.

    g. Find a compatible roommate.

    h. Get a parking pass.

    i. Select a major.

    When you write the essay, remember that your audience will be new freshmen, your role will be that of an advisor, and your purpose will be to inform freshmen so they are better able to cope with campus life.

2. The administration of your university is concerned about drinking on your campus. You are president of student government and have been asked to help prepare an alcohol policy aimed at reducing underage drinking and at promoting responsible drinking among those of legal

age who choose to drink. You can include ideas for regulations, education, disciplinary policies, and anything else you care to address. Your audience will be campus administrators, your role will be that of knowledgeable student, and your purpose will be to help develop a policy to reduce unsafe and illegal drinking practices on your campus and to persuade administrators to adopt your ideas.

3. A big birthday bash is being planned for someone you respect and care a great deal for (pick anyone you regard highly—a friend, a relative, a teacher, a coach, a member of the clergy). You have been asked to write a character sketch of the person that presents and illustrates one or two of the person's best traits. Mention the trait or traits and go on to give examples that illustrate the trait(s). The sketch will be photocopied and distributed to everyone in attendance. Your audience will be people who also know and care for the person, your role will be that of an admirer, and your purpose will be to praise the person by sharing impressions and experiences.

4. You are a member of the local Chamber of Commerce, which is putting together a brochure to promote tourism in your area. Pick a spot in your area (a recreational spot, a historic area, an educational place, an amusement spot) and write a description of it to be included in the brochure. Your audience is the traveler looking for a place to spend some time, your purpose is to persuade the person to visit your area, and your role is that of someone who takes pride in the spot you are describing.

5. For the last week you have been home with the flu, and to pass the time you have watched a great deal of television. The programming aimed at children, you have noticed, is unsatisfactory: The shows and accompanying commercials are manipulative, aimed at getting children to pester their parents for toys and sugared food. Write a letter of protest to the networks to persuade them to improve the quality of shows and commercials aimed at children. Your role is that of a concerned citizen.

6. When you were in high school, you were the editor of the school newspaper. Now your alma mater is planning a press day, and you have been asked to deliver a speech that expresses whether or not you believe high school principals should be permitted to censor the contents of high school publications. Your audience will be the newspaper and yearbook staffs; your purpose will be to persuade your audience to adopt your view; your role is that of a former high school journalist keenly interested in censorship issues.

7. Congratulations! You are the winner of a writing contest. Your prize is the opportunity to have a 500- to 700-word essay published in the magazine of your choice. You may write on any topic and for any purpose.

Just be sure your material is suitable for the readers of whatever magazine you choose.

8. As a guest columnist for your campus newspaper, you plan to write an article about an important campus issue: diversity, grading policies, degree requirements, extracurricular programming, or some other issue. Your role is that of concerned student, your audience is the campus community, and your goal is to convince readers to share your view.

9. You have recently begun an e-mail correspondence with someone who lives in another country. He or she has asked that you describe American life as honestly and precisely as possible. Pick one aspect, such as shopping, dating, college life, high school, or presidential politics, and write a thorough description for someone who knows very little about this country. Your purpose is to inform, and your role is that of an ambassador and teacher.

10. Pick a controversial issue and write a letter to the editor of your town newspaper expressing your view on the issue. Your audience is the readers of the newspaper, your purpose is to persuade them to think or act in accordance with your view, and your role is that of a concerned citizen.

11. You are a member of the local school board. Recently, a number of parents have complained because commencement ceremonies traditionally begin with a nondenominational prayer. Although no particular religion is represented by the prayer, these parents maintain that any prayer is inappropriate because it violates the separation of church and state guaranteed by the Constitution. Furthermore, these parents maintain that the rights of atheists are violated by the prayer. Do you support the view of these parents? Write a position paper that either recommends abolishing the prayer or recommends retaining it, and support your stand. Your audience is the rest of the school board, and your purpose is to convince them to take the course of action you recommend.

12. As part of a job application, you have been asked to write a character sketch of yourself that presents and illustrates your chief strengths and weaknesses. Your audience is the personnel director, your purpose is to present a realistic yet favorable portrait, and your role is that of job applicant.

13. If you have a job, assume that your boss has asked you to write a report that describes one change that could be made to improve efficiency, morale, or profitability. You are to explain the change, why it is needed, and how it would improve operations. Your audience is the chief management person, your purpose is to persuade this person to institute the change, and your role is that of a dedicated employee.

14. You are taking a study skills class, and your instructor has assigned a paper that requires you to classify and describe the study habits of students. To research this paper, interview as many students as necessary to discover how they study, how much they study, when they study, and where they study. Your audience is your instructor, your purpose is to inform, and your role is that of a student who wants to do well in the course.

15. You are taking a psychology course, and to help you appreciate how people are affected by events in their lives, your instructor has asked you to write an essay that explains how some event in your life has affected you (a death, a divorce, making a game-winning touchdown, being cut from a team, being class president, failing a test, moving to a new town, getting a speeding ticket, and so on). Your instructor has asked that you write the essay for someone you feel close to in order to share a significant part of your life. Your role is that of close friend or relative of your reader.

Coping with Essay Examinations

The tips in this section may help you improve your performance on essay examinations. Of course, there is no substitute for thorough studying, so the tips only work if you are prepared. If you think you need to sharpen your study skills, visit your campus study skills center.

Understand the Value of Anxiety

Because anxiety can keep you alert and focused so you perform well, if you are nervous before and during an exam, you should not be concerned. However, while a degree of anxiety will help you, too much can make you panicky and hurt your performance. To keep your anxiety at the appropriate level, use the test-taking strategies in this appendix.

Have a Test-Taking Plan

A plan helps you keep your anxiety in check because it tells you what you will do first, second, third, and so forth. When you know how you will proceed, you minimize the anxiety and fear associated with the unknown. If you need a plan, try this:

1. Read through the entire test to understand what is expected of you.

2. Decide how you will budget your time. If you have one hour to answer four questions, plan to spend 15 minutes on each question. If some questions are worth more points than others, spend the most time on the questions worth the most points.

3. Plan your first answer with a scratch outline. Make a quick list of the points you will cover, and number them in the order you will write them up.

4. Write your first answer, using your scratch outline. Do not plan to revise; you may not have time.

5. Outline and write your next answer, and proceed in this manner until you have completed the test.

6. If you have time after answering all the questions, go back and revise as necessary.

ORGANIZE SIMPLY

Time is not on your side, so forget elaborate introductions and conclusions. Open with a thesis that reflects the question and go on to make your points. For example, if the question is "Explain manifest destiny," begin this way: "Manifest destiny is. . . ."

ANSWER THE QUESTIONS YOU ARE SURE OF FIRST

While you are answering the questions you know, a portion of your brain will turn to the ones you are less certain of, and the answers you need may occur to you.

THINK POSITIVELY

All things being equal, positive thinkers outperform negative thinkers.

PICTURE YOURSELF TAKING THE TEST

If you become overly anxious about tests, repeatedly picture yourself in the classroom, receiving the exam sheet, reading it over, writing scratch outlines, answering questions successfully, and feeling confident.

AVOID PADDING YOUR ANSWERS

Your instructor will recognize padding (adding unrelated information because you do not know the correct answer). A busy instructor will be annoyed by it, and you do not want to annoy the person giving you a grade.

IF YOU DO NOT KNOW THE ANSWER, GUESS

If you are lucky, you may get some points. Guessing is not the same as padding, however. Keep your answer, whether or not it is a guess, to the point.

IF YOU RUN OUT OF TIME, MAKE A LIST OF THE POINTS YOU WOULD HAVE INCLUDED IN YOUR ANSWER

Most instructors will give at least partial credit if you demonstrate your knowledge.

WEAR A WATCH

You need to keep track of the time so you know how long to spend on each answer.

IF YOU DO NOT UNDERSTAND A QUESTION, ASK YOUR INSTRUCTOR FOR CLARIFICATION

You may not get help, but then again you may.

INDEX